The
Daily
BIBLE PROMISE
BOOK®

The *Daily* BIBLE PROMISE BOOK®

A 365-Day Devotional &
Bible Reading Plan

BARBOUR BOOKS
An Imprint of Barbour Publishing, Inc.

© 2013 by Barbour Publishing, Inc.

Text previously appeared in *The KJV Daily Promise Bible*, published by Barbour Publishing.

Print ISBN 978-1-68322-441-9

eBook Editions:
Adobe Digital Edition (.epub) 978-1-68322-677-2
Kindle and MobiPocket Edition (.prc) 978-1-68322-678-9

All scripture quotations are taken from the King James Version of the Bible.

Cover photograph: Mission Media, Lightstock

Published by Barbour Books, an imprint of Barbour Publishing, Inc., 1810 Barbour Drive, Uhrichsville, Ohio 44683, www.barbourbooks.com

Our mission is to inspire the world with the life-changing message of the Bible.

Member of the
Evangelical Christian
Publishers Association

Printed in the United States of America.

INTRODUCTION

Many people would like to read through the Bible in a year—but we know, from personal experience, that can be a real challenge. That's why we created *The Daily Bible Promise Book*®—to give you the encouragement you need as you begin this life-changing journey.

In addition to daily scripture readings for every day of the year—an Old Testament, New Testament, and either Psalms or Proverbs passage—this book also features 365 challenging and encouraging devotional thoughts, each highlighting a particular Bible promise from that day's scripture selection.

Each day's reading should take 15 to 30 minutes to complete. If you stay with it, you'll soon be able to say, "I read through the Bible in a year!"—and you'll undoubtedly find your life changed by the great promises of God's Word.

The Publisher

Bible reading:

GENESIS 1–2; MATTHEW 1; PSALM 1

And the LORD God said,
It is not good that the man should be alone;
I will make him an help meet for him.

GENESIS 2:18

This promise to one man, Adam, is also a promise to people in general—that in marriage they will find a helper that is right for them. But for everyone—even those men and women who never marry—God will provide a Helper in His Holy Spirit (John 15:26), who gives Christians the power they need to live well (Galatians 5:22–23).

GENESIS 3–4; MATTHEW 2; PSALM 2

And thou Bethlehem, in the land of Juda,
art not the least among the princes of Juda:
for out of thee shall come a Governor,
that shall rule my people Israel.

MATTHEW 2:6

The Jewish leaders, in answering King Herod's question, were quoting the prophet Micah, who predicted Jesus' birth—and birthplace—more than seven hundred years earlier. You can be sure that when God makes a promise, He'll keep it!

Bible reading:

GENESIS 5–7; MATTHEW 3; PSALM 3

But thou, O LORD,
art a shield for me; my glory,
and the lifter up of mine head.

PSALM 3:3

Like a mother chicken, wrapping her wings around her little ones (Matthew 23:37), God protects and cares for His own. Though we still experience troubles in this world—accidents, illnesses, ultimately death—we know that God will never leave us on our own (Hebrews 13:5), and He is preparing an eternal home for us (John 14:2).

Bible reading:

GENESIS 8–10; MATTHEW 4; PSALM 4

But [Jesus] answered and said,
It is written, Man shall not live by bread alone,
but by every word that proceedeth
out of the mouth of God.

MATTHEW 4:4

Want to find real life? It's in the living and powerful Word of God (Hebrews 4:12). You need bread to feed your body, but the Bible gives strength to your soul and spirit. You're now in the fourth day of a one-year "diet" of God's Word—stay with it! This is where you'll find the life worth living.

Bible reading:

GENESIS 11–13; MATTHEW 5:1–20; PSALM 5

*Now the LORD had said unto Abram, Get thee out of
thy country, and from thy kindred, and from thy father's
house, unto a land that I will shew thee: And I will make
of thee a great nation, and I will bless thee, and make
thy name great; and thou shalt be a blessing.*

GENESIS 12:1–2

Over some four thousand years, God has proven
that His promises are good. God changed Abram's
name, which means "honored father," to *Abraham*—
"father of many"—and Abraham is the forefather
of the Jewish people. But he's also the father of
those who believe God by faith (Romans 4:16)—a
great heavenly nation from among all the people
of earth!

Bible reading:

GENESIS 14–16; MATTHEW 5:21–48; PSALM 6

*But I say unto you, Love your enemies, bless them
that curse you, do good to them that hate you,
and pray for them which despitefully use you,
and persecute you; That ye may be the children
of your Father which is in heaven.*

MATTHEW 5:44–45

If you want to be sure you're saved, Jesus gives a test in this verse: Are you praying for those people who treat you badly? If you are, Jesus says you're a son (or daughter) of the heavenly Father. It's not always easy, humanly speaking, but God has also promised that "my strength is made perfect in weakness" (2 Corinthians 12:9).

Bible reading:

GENESIS 17–18; MATTHEW 6:1–18; PSALM 7

God judgeth the righteous.

PSALM 7:11

We live in an unfair world. The wealthy and powerful seem to work the system to their own ends, leaving the rest of us craving justice. But the psalm writer promises that God's judgments are right and sure. Since God knows everything (1 John 3:20), He can decide who's right, who's wrong, and what's best. Be faithful—and trust Him with the end result.

DAY 8

GENESIS 19–20; MATTHEW 6:19–34; PSALM 8

*But seek ye first the kingdom of God,
and his righteousness; and all these
things shall be added unto you.*

MATTHEW 6:33

Sometimes life seems incomplete unless we have something to worry about. What will happen if. . . ? What am I going to do about. . . ? How can I afford. . . ? In Matthew 6, Jesus offers a simple dose of reality: God feeds the birds and dresses the grass. Of course He's going to provide for His children. So don't worry—trust.

Bible reading:

GENESIS 21–23; MATTHEW 7:1–11; PSALM 9:1–8

And the LORD visited Sarah as he had said,
and the LORD did unto Sarah as he had spoken.

GENESIS 21:1

Crazy as it seemed, ninety-year-old Sarah was having a baby. Why? Because God had promised her husband, Abraham, that he would become the father of a great nation—and God always keeps His promises, even those that may seem impossible. Or, in God's own words, "Is any thing too hard for the LORD?" (Genesis 18:14).

Bible reading:

GENESIS 24; MATTHEW 7:12–29; PSALM 9:9–20

*Therefore whosoever heareth these sayings of mine,
and doeth them, I will liken him unto a wise man,
which built his house upon a rock.*

MATTHEW 7:24

God doesn't want you to simply be a silent partner.
To have a faith that's lasting, you can't just talk
the talk. . .you've got to walk the talk. The apostle
James puts it another way: "But be ye doers of the
word, and not hearers only, deceiving your own
selves" (James 1:22). God promises your faith will
be stronger if you really live your life for Him.

Bible reading:

Genesis 25–26; Matthew 8:1–17; Psalm 10:1–11

*That it might be fulfilled which was spoken
by Esaias the prophet, saying, Himself took
our infirmities, and bare our sicknesses.*

Matthew 8:17

Sickness, the death of a loved one, the loss of a job, marital problems. . . As Christians, we all struggle with faith in those trying times of our lives. It's not always easy to give up control to God. But He has promised to care for us—always. Remember that God will never forsake you (Hebrews 13:5), and hold fast to faith. If God says it, He'll do it!

Bible reading:

GENESIS 27:1–28:9; MATTHEW 8:18–34;
PSALM 10:12–18

*Thou hast seen it; for thou beholdest mischief and spite,
to requite it with thy hand: the poor committeth himself
unto thee; thou art the helper of the fatherless.*

PSALM 10:14

As Creator, heavenly Father, Savior, and Lord,
God is the most versatile character on the stage of
life. When an important player in life—a mom, a
dad, a mentor, a friend—is missing, God steps in
and knows all the right lines and cues. The truth
is, human relationships fail to meet expectations.
A relationship with God will never fall short of
the mark.

Bible reading:

And, behold, the LORD stood above it, and said,
I am the LORD God of Abraham thy father,
and the God of Isaac: the land whereon thou liest,
to thee will I give it, and to thy seed.

GENESIS 28:13

❖━━■□■━━❖

Ever wonder why the tiny nation of Israel—about the size and population of Massachusetts—is such a focal point for world events? Today's verse helps to explain. God promised Jacob (later renamed "Israel") that his family would always have claim to land in the Middle East. Though for centuries many have fought these "chosen people" (Deuteronomy 10:15), Israel's presence proves God's faithfulness.

Bible reading:

GENESIS 30:1–31:21; MATTHEW 10:1–15; PSALM 12

*Thou shalt keep them, O LORD,
thou shalt preserve them from this
generation for ever.*

PSALM 12:7

Our world is overflowing with temptations, which constantly try to lay claim to our hearts and minds. We can rejoice in knowing that our Lord and Savior has provided us with His protection and strength when our human desires threaten to take over, when our own strength just isn't enough. He is faithful (2 Thessalonians 3:3)!

*Whosoever therefore shall confess me before men,
him will I confess also before my Father
which is in heaven.*

MATTHEW 10:32

It's a simple, give-and-take transaction. Tell others about Jesus on earth and Jesus tells His Father in heaven. Harvesting the fruit of sharing Christ with others may seem like its own reward, but Jesus offers more. Like a proud parent, He brags on His followers for an everlasting reward.

Bible reading:

GENESIS 32:22–34:31; MATTHEW 10:37–11:6;
PSALM 14

He that findeth his life shall lose it:
and he that loseth his life for my sake shall find it.

MATTHEW 10:39

Here is a paradox—a seemingly contradictory statement. But Jesus wasn't just playing with words. He knew that real life—life in the Spirit on earth, life forever in heaven—comes only when people surrender everything to Him. "I am the way, the truth, and the life," Jesus said (John 14:6). His new life (1 Corinthians 15:22) is better than anything we could lose!

*Lord, who shall abide in thy tabernacle?
who shall dwell in thy holy hill? He that walketh
uprightly, and worketh righteousness,
and speaketh the truth in his heart.*

PSALM 15:1–2

Christlike. This word brings to mind the ultimate goal of the Christian life—to be more like Jesus every day. While we'll never be perfect because of our sinful human nature, we can strive for righteous living. . .taking a stand for what's good and acceptable in God's sight (Romans 12:2). Then we can enjoy an ever-growing, intimate relationship with Christ—for life!

Bible reading:

*Come unto me, all ye that labour
and are heavy laden, and I will give you rest.*
Matthew 11:28

Life has a way of dragging down, tiring out, and frustrating even the most able-bodied people. Relationships, careers, responsibilities, burdens, and unexpected troubles weigh heavily on hearts and minds, often pulling committed believers away from building a relationship with Christ. But He knows we're busy, overworked, and tired. That's why He promises us rest—more satisfying than the best nap ever—if we simply go to Him.

Bible reading:

GENESIS 39–40; MATTHEW 12:1–29; PSALM 17

Behold my servant, whom I have chosen; my beloved, in whom my soul is well pleased: I will put my spirit upon him, and he shall shew judgment to the Gentiles.

MATTHEW 12:18

Good parents give their children boundaries—a clear understanding of what should and shouldn't be done. God did the same for everyone through Jesus. Today's verse, a quotation from the Old Testament's book of Isaiah (42:1), describes One who will help the world understand right and wrong. Many won't accept Jesus' teaching, but those of us who do can enjoy the protection of God's perfect boundaries.

Bible reading:

GENESIS 41; MATTHEW 12:30–50; PSALM 18:1–15

For whosoever shall do the will of my Father
which is in heaven, the same is my
brother, and sister, and mother.

MATTHEW 12:50

When we take time to walk in Jesus' steps, we can feel closer to Him than ever before. We don't have to earn a degree in theology or travel to a remote mission outpost to be part of Jesus' family. Such a small gesture as giving someone a drink of cold water (Matthew 10:42) is worthy of blessing. Jesus said, "Freely ye have received, freely give" (Matthew 10:8).

Bible reading:

GENESIS 42–43; MATTHEW 13:1–9; PSALM 18:16–29

For thou wilt light my candle:
the LORD my God will enlighten my darkness.
PSALM 18:28

Life often seems too hard, and maybe occasionally even downright hopeless. When your light seems to be growing dim in the shadows of sin and sorrow, look up. Our Lord is the only real source of joy and hope there is. Lean on Him; He will keep your light burning bright.

Bible reading:

Genesis 44–45; Matthew 13:10–23;
Psalm 18:30–50

---

*For whosoever hath, to him shall be given, and he shall
have more abundance: but whosoever hath not,
from him shall be taken away even that he hath.*

Matthew 13:12

The disciples once asked Jesus why He liked to speak in parables—picture-stories with hidden meanings. Jesus' answer was a promise of spiritual insight for anyone who truly knows Him. When we believe in Jesus, God gives us a supernatural ability to understand the Bible and apply it to our lives. And it's not just a *little* ability, it's more than enough for the job. That's always the way God gives—over and above.

Bible reading:

GENESIS 46:1–47:26; MATTHEW 13:24–43; PSALM 19

The law of the LORD is perfect, converting the soul:
the testimony of the LORD is sure, making wise the simple.

PSALM 19:7

This world can be a depressing place, with daily reports of wars, disasters, and terrorism. Sometimes it's just as bad on the personal level, as people struggle with finances, disease, and relationships. But God promises a safe haven, a place to find new strength for the soul: His Word. The Bible is "quick, and powerful" (Hebrews 4:12). Take advantage of its benefits today!

Bible reading:

Genesis 47:27–49:28; Matthew 13:44–58;
Psalm 20

Now know I that the LORD saveth his anointed;
he will hear him from his holy heaven with
the saving strength of his right hand.

Psalm 20:6

We trust our friends. We trust our spouses. We trust our coworkers. We trust people who will inevitably let us down from time to time. Imagine how much more we can lean on our Savior, who keeps every one of His promises to us! Start today and put your trust in the only One who guarantees He'll never disappoint you—that's a promise!

Bible reading:

And Joseph said unto his brethren, I die: and God will surely visit you, and bring you out of this land unto the land which he sware to Abraham, to Isaac, and to Jacob.

GENESIS 50:24

The sons of Jacob didn't deserve the kind treatment their brother Joseph extended to them. After selling Joseph into Egyptian slavery and telling Jacob his beloved son was dead, Joseph's brothers folded their arms in smug pride of getting rid of the favored child. But later, after Joseph saved the entire family from famine and certain death, Joseph even went as far as to assure his family that God would indeed take care of them—the same way He takes care of His children today.

And God heard their groaning, and God remembered his covenant with Abraham, with Isaac, and with Jacob.

EXODUS 2:24

Under Joseph, the Jewish slave boy turned ruler, Egypt welcomed the people of Israel. But when a new king made life hard for the Jews, they cried to God—and He remembered His agreement with Abraham, Isaac, and Jacob. In time, God would lead the people back to their own land, just as He'd promised. Today, be sure that He'll also remember the promises He's made to *you.*

Bible reading:

EXODUS 4:1–5:21; MATTHEW 15:29–16:12;
PSALM 22:22–31

*For he hath not despised nor abhorred the affliction
of the afflicted; neither hath he hid his face from him;
but when he cried unto him, he heard.*

PSALM 22:24

❖ ━━━━ ❖

Have you ever turned your eyes and heart away
from someone in need? Have you ever ignored a
plea for help? Follow Jesus' example from today's
scripture, and listen to the cries of those who are
hurting. Whether you are able to give financial
or emotional support, or even just a few hours
of your time, you're promised to be blessed for
your efforts.

Bible reading:

EXODUS 5:22–7:24; MATTHEW 16:13–28; PSALM 23

And I say also unto thee, That thou art Peter,
and upon this rock I will build my church;
and the gates of hell shall not prevail against it.

MATTHEW 16:18

During His ministry, Jesus Christ laid the groundwork for the kingdom of God on earth— the church. His disciples, although devoted to their leader, must have looked at each other with skepticism that such an institution could be built on their shoulders. But Jesus promises more than an organization of believers. Someday, when all other earthly institutions fail, Christ's church will live on.

Bible reading:

Exodus 7:25–9:35; Matthew 17:1–9; Psalm 24

*And Pharaoh said, I will let you go, that ye may
sacrifice to the LORD your God in the wilderness.*
Exodus 8:28

Here's an example of a human promise—the kind
you *can't* count on. The king of Egypt said he would
let Moses and the people of Israel leave their
slavery, but then he changed his mind. Isn't it nice
to know that God never goes back on a promise?
"God is not a man, that he should lie; neither the
son of man, that he should repent: hath he said,
and shall he not do it? or hath he spoken, and
shall he not make it good?" (Numbers 23:19).

Bible reading:

Exodus 10–11; Matthew 17:10–27; Psalm 25

Mine eyes are ever toward the LORD;
for he shall pluck my feet out of the net.
PSALM 25:15

❖————❖

Today, while we don't think of our feet being tangled in a net, we *can* imagine being stuck in a rut, going nowhere fast, or getting caught up in the rat race. Whatever the euphemism, our lives are truly hopeless without the knowledge of Jesus' saving grace and the hope of eternal life. Keep your eyes on Jesus, knowing He has a plan for you (Hebrews 12:1–2).

Bible reading:

Exodus 12; Matthew 18:1–20; Psalm 26

For the Son of man is come to
save that which was lost.
Matthew 18:11

Never has a greater gift been given, the gift of God's Son. . .who was sent to save us from sin and to offer eternal life (John 3:16). He was sent to save the "lost." We don't have to be perfect and sin-free. We can't purchase eternal life, because it's a gift freely given. All we need to do is believe God's promise and accept this gift. It doesn't get any easier than that!

Bible reading:

Exodus 13–14; Matthew 18:21–35; Psalm 27

When my father and my mother forsake me,
then the LORD will take me up.

Psalm 27:10

Earthly relationships often fall apart. Families separate. Parents abandon their children. Friends come and go. But we need not ever feel lost and forgotten. We have the Lord, who will always be close to our hearts. A Father who will always listen, always support, always care. Lean on Him, and you'll never be lonely. That's a promise!

Bible reading:

Exodus 15–16; Matthew 19:1–15; Psalm 28

*For this cause shall a man leave father and mother,
and shall cleave to his wife: and they
twain shall be one flesh.*

MATTHEW 19:5

God's promise for marriage is that it will be unlike any other relationship between two people. The Bible describes friendship or brotherhood as being *near* one another (Proverbs 18:24). But in a marriage, husband and wife are not just joined, they experience a oneness in Christ. Think of it as preparation for perfect harmony with God that's only attainable in eternity.

Bible reading:

EXODUS 17–19; MATTHEW 19:16–30; PSALM 29

*But Jesus beheld them, and said unto them, With men
this is impossible; but with God all things are possible.*
MATTHEW 19:26

Forget silly questions like, "Can God create a rock
so big that He can't lift it?" God won't ever do
anything that goes against His nature—but He can
do anything that benefits you as His child. "If ye
then, being evil, know how to give good gifts unto
your children," Jesus once said, "how much more
shall your heavenly Father give the Holy Spirit to
them that ask him?" (Luke 11:13).

Bible reading

EXODUS 20–21; MATTHEW 20:1–19; PSALM 30

*And shewing mercy unto thousands of them
that love me, and keep my commandments.*
EXODUS 20:6

❖━━━◆◆◆━━━❖

Ever been asked what makes you seem so different?
Why you're able to get through tough times
without breaking? Share the good news that Christ
has blessed you and that He makes it possible to
have joy in *all* stages of life—even the not-so-good
times. When you serve the Lord, your light will
shine (Matthew 5:16), and His delight will bring
abundant blessings to you. So much that others
will take notice.

*And whosoever will be chief among you,
let him be your servant.*

Matthew 20:27

Jesus leads the campaign for upside-down, topsy-turvy, counterintuitive rules for His kingdom. Instead of the best getting first dibs, it's the lowliest among His followers—those willing to serve others the same way Christ served—that will one day earn a place of honor in eternity.

Bible reading:

EXODUS 24–25; MATTHEW 21:1–27; PSALM 31:9–18

And all things, whatsoever ye shall ask in prayer,
believing, ye shall receive.

MATTHEW 21:22

❖

Faith connects us to God. When we really believe in who He is and what He's promised, He responds with all the power in the universe— because that's exactly what God is. When our faith-filled prayers align with His desires, look out. Amazing things are about to happen!

Bible reading:

EXODUS 26–27; MATTHEW 21:28–46;
PSALM 31:19–24

O love the LORD, all ye his saints:
for the LORD preserveth the faithful.

PSALM 31:23

Walk beside the Lord, and you'll reap the benefits of serving Him. He'll reward you if you earnestly seek Him (Hebrews 11:6). He'll give you what you ask for in prayer (Matthew 21:22). He'll bless your life (John 20:29). Be faithful, and you're sure to experience an amazing life—guaranteed.

DAY 39

I acknowledge my sin unto thee, and mine iniquity
have I not hid. I said, I will confess my
transgressions unto the LORD; and thou
forgavest the iniquity of my sin.

PSALM 32:5

God's forgiveness offers much more than removal
of sin. In addition to wiping clean a repenting
sinner's slate, He removes the guilt of the offense.
Just think—it isn't necessary to dwell on, regret,
or stew about forgiven sin. It's God's guarantee—
designed to calm His children's spirits and to
bless their lives.

DAY 40

Bible reading:

EXODUS 29; MATTHEW 23:1–36; PSALM 33:1–12

*The counsel of the LORD standeth for ever,
the thoughts of his heart to all generations.*

PSALM 33:11

"I've had a change of plans." Is there anyone who has *never* spoken those words or had them spoken to them? Human life is all about change—but God offers beautiful security in His never-changing plans. Like what? How about Jesus' plans on heaven: "And if I go and prepare a place for you, I will come again, and receive you unto myself; that where I am, there ye may be also" (John 14:3).

DAY 41

Bible reading:

EXODUS 30–31; MATTHEW 23:37–24:28;
PSALM 33:13–22

*Six days may work be done; but in the seventh is the
sabbath of rest, holy to the LORD. . .for in six days
the LORD made heaven and earth, and on the
seventh day he rested, and was refreshed.*

EXODUS 31:15, 17

Rest is an important concept in the Bible. Besides
God's example after Creation, we read about
the land needing a rest from constant planting
(Leviticus 25:5) and Jesus needing to rest after
dealing with throngs of people (Mark 6:31). God
knows that when we rest, when we are still, we
are most able to sense His presence in our lives.
Spend some time resting in God's promise today.

Bible reading:

EXODUS 32–33; MATTHEW 24:29–51; PSALM 34:1–7

I sought the LORD, and he heard me,
and delivered me from all my fears.
PSALM 34:4

Give honor and glory to God by placing your worries at His feet. He alone offers all the comfort and assurance we need for whatever we're facing in our lives. Without Him, we'd be anxious, we'd be afraid, we'd be hopeless. . .but with Him, we can be at peace, knowing He is all we'll ever need. He will give us rest from the burdens of life (Matthew 11:28).

Bible reading:

Watch therefore, for ye know neither the day nor the hour wherein the Son of man cometh.

Matthew 25:13

Humans thrive on being in control. Schedules, agendas, and calendars can spell out every minute of every day. But Jesus Christ left the date and time of His return a mystery. The Son Himself doesn't even know when He'll make his next earthly appearance (Matthew 24:36). Christians shouldn't take this uncertainty and push the panic button. Instead, consider waiting in expectant anticipation, preparing each day as though Jesus will return.

Bible reading:

EXODUS 35:30–37:29; MATTHEW 25:14–30;
PSALM 35:1–8

---

*Draw out also the spear, and stop the way
against them that persecute me: say unto
my soul, I am thy salvation.*

PSALM 35:3

The psalm writer was upset. Enemies were pursuing him with murder on their minds. But the ancient poet knew just where to find deliverance: from the one true God, the only One able to save. Times and circumstances have changed since this psalm was written, but God is still in the saving business. "As ye have therefore received Christ Jesus the Lord, so walk ye in him" (Colossians 2:6).

Bible reading:

Exodus 38–39; Matthew 25:31–46;
Psalm 35:9–17

And the King shall answer and say unto them,
Verily I say unto you, Inasmuch as ye have done
it unto one of the least of these my brethren,
ye have done it unto me.

Matthew 25:40

God calls on us to love each other—just as He loves us (John 13:34). Today's scripture tells us more about loving those who may not be living up to our standards in the world. For every deed of kindness, every hand reached out in love, comes the reminder that we are reflecting these actions onto Christ. Loving others—even those who are unlovable to the rest of the world—delights our heavenly Father. Let your light shine!

Bible reading:

EXODUS 40; MATTHEW 26:1–35; PSALM 35:18–28

For this is my blood of the new testament,
which is shed for many for the remission of sins.
MATTHEW 26:28

Countless songs and poems have been written about the blood of Jesus. The beauty of forgiveness through Christ's blood is undeniable—yet the pain, suffering, and sacrifice He experienced shouldn't be overlooked. Jesus of Nazareth was a man of flesh and bones just like us. His painful death would have been worth it to Him, even if only one person ever accepted the gift.

Bible reading:

LEVITICUS 1–3; MATTHEW 26:36–68; PSALM 36:1–6

Jesus saith unto him, Thou hast said:
nevertheless I say unto you, Hereafter shall ye see the
Son of man sitting on the right hand of power,
and coming in the clouds of heaven.

MATTHEW 26:64

❧

Here is one of the most exciting promises in all of God's Word: Jesus is coming again! Once He came to earth quietly, as a helpless baby in a small-town stable. But the day is coming when He'll reappear as a powerful King. When will that be? It's a surprise, according to Jesus Himself: "Watch therefore: for ye know not what hour your Lord doth come" (Matthew 24:42).

DAY 48

Bible reading:

LEVITICUS 4:1–5:13; MATTHEW 26:69–27:26;
PSALM 36:7–12

*They shall be abundantly satisfied with the fatness
of thy house; and thou shalt make them
drink of the river of thy pleasures.*

PSALM 36:8

If your heart's lacking joy today, drink deep from
God's promise (Psalm 37:4). Just knowing that
He holds our lives in the palm of His hand is
reason enough to rejoice—no matter what the day
might bring. Thank Him for His mercy and His
everlasting goodness. Nothing else in the world
can bring joy into our lives like He can.

Bible reading:

LEVITICUS 5:14–7:21; MATTHEW 27:27–50;
PSALM 37:1–6

*Delight thyself also in the LORD: and he shall
give thee the desires of thine heart.*

PSALM 37:4

❧——◆——❧

Ask a child to make a Christmas list and he won't
struggle to come up with a lengthy collection of
wants. Adults, too, have a hard time distinguishing
between needs and wants. It's easy to read Psalm
37:4 to mean Christians get whatever they want—
making God little more than a glorified Santa
Claus. But it's much more than that. "Delighting
in the Lord" means allowing His perfect wisdom
to transform a heart desire to what ultimately
brings His kingdom to earth.

Bible reading:

Leviticus 7:22–8:36; Matthew 27:51–66;
Psalm 37:7–26

For yet a little while, and the wicked shall not be:
yea, thou shalt diligently consider his
place, and it shall not be.

Psalm 37:10

"The sinful man" has caused plenty of trouble in our world—terrorism, child abuse, murder, even the business scandals that wipe out jobs and retirement funds. But the psalm writer knew a day was coming when God would take every evil influence out of the picture. In "a little while," from God's eternal viewpoint, sin will be gone—replaced by the perfection of heaven (Revelation 21:4).

DAY 51

Bible reading:

LEVITICUS 9–10; MATTHEW 28; PSALM 37:27–40

*And the angel answered and said unto the women,
Fear not ye: for I know that ye seek Jesus, which was
crucified. He is not here: for he is risen, as he said.
Come, see the place where the Lord lay.*

MATTHEW 28:5–6

Of all the promises in the Bible, surely none is more treasured than Jesus' assurance that He would rise from the dead. Because Jesus conquered death, we, too, will live forever with Him—if only we believe that He is God's Son. Want to dispel those winter blues? Start your day by praising God for His most wonderful Son. . .and know that one day you'll meet Him face-to-face.

Bible reading:

LEVITICUS 11–12; MARK 1:1–28; PSALM 38

For in thee, O LORD, do I hope:
thou wilt hear, O Lord my God.

PSALM 38:15

Waiting. . . It's not easy to wait for an answer to prayer. Sometimes we feel like we've been placed on hold—or maybe God has even forgotten our request. We can rest assured that He *will* answer our prayer—God's Word says we just need to be patient (Psalm 37:7). He knows what's best for us. His timing—even though it may not be what we had in mind—is always perfect.

And now, Lord, what wait I for?
my hope is in thee.
PSALM 39:7

Nothing on earth is certain. Plans can be made, provisions supplied, money saved, and schedules penned, but none of these is guaranteed. The healthiest relationship can fail, and leaders fall from grace. When everything seems to crumble, count on hope in God—the Author, Savior, and Friend above all. His plan for eternity is a guarantee for Christians.

DAY 54

❖ *Bible reading:* ❖

Leviticus 14; Mark 1:40–2:12; Psalm 40:1–8

*When Jesus saw their faith, he said unto the sick
of the palsy, Son, thy sins be forgiven thee.*

Mark 2:5

Two thousand years ago, Jesus made this life-changing promise to a man with a great need. He's still speaking those words. "If we confess our sins, he is faithful and just to forgive us our sins, and to cleanse us from all unrighteousness," the apostle John wrote (1 John 1:9). With our sins forgiven, we are truly God's sons and daughters, enjoying all the benefits of that wonderful relationship.

Bible reading:

LEVITICUS 15; MARK 2:13–3:35; PSALM 40:9–17

*For whosoever shall do the will of God, the same is
my brother, and my sister, and mother.*

MARK 3:35

A member of Jesus' family. That's what He calls
you if you are a follower of God. You belong to
a much larger family than that of your father,
mother, sisters, and brothers. You are a part
of a body (a *family*) of believers (Romans 12:5)—
your "brothers" and "sisters" in Christ. Today,
celebrate and thank the Lord for this extended
family.

Bible reading:

LEVITICUS 16–17; MARK 4:1–20; PSALM 41:1–4

Blessed is he that considereth the poor:
the LORD will deliver him in time of trouble.

PSALM 41:1

❖━━━━❖

Jesus had a special place in His heart for the earth's poor. Throughout His earthly ministry He urged His followers to take care of the less fortunate, clothe the bare, and feed the hungry. Here the psalm writer says that caring for the poor not only brings happiness, but that the Lord promises the giver a safety net during the rough patches of life.

Bible reading:

LEVITICUS 18–19; MARK 4:21–41; PSALM 41:5–13

Ye shall therefore keep my statutes,
and my judgments: which if a man do,
he shall live in them: I am the LORD.

LEVITICUS 18:5

Why, some people ask, does God have so many rules? Is He trying to take away all our fun? Hardly. God's laws are designed both to honor Him and to protect us. Compare today's Old Testament passage with the realities of the modern world—pornography, AIDS, sexual abuse, broken families. Can anyone honestly argue that God's ways are too restrictive?

*Yet the LORD will command his lovingkindness in the day
time, and in the night his song shall be with me,
and my prayer unto the God of my life.*

PSALM 42:8

A friend, a faithful companion, a loving
Father—24-7. He's by your side, offering you
His comfort, His kindness, His mercy. . . . There
isn't a moment, day or night, that He'll leave you
on your own. No matter what time of day, you can
go to Him in prayer and He'll be ready to listen,
wrapping His loving arms around you.

Bible reading:

LEVITICUS 21–22; MARK 6:1–13; PSALM 44

Through thee will we push down our enemies:
through thy name will we tread them
under that rise up against us.

PSALM 44:5

❖ ⋯ ❖

God doesn't promise a life free of enemies. Jesus tells His followers in Matthew 5:44 to "Love your enemies, bless them that curse you, do good to them that hate you, and pray for them which despitefully use you, and persecute you." He even guarantees persecution to Christians (Matthew 24:9). But these promises aren't all doom and gloom. The heavenly Father says His followers will be able to overcome their enemies in ultimate victory—victory that was sealed when Jesus gave His life on the cross.

❧ *Bible reading:*

LEVITICUS 23–24; MARK 6:14–29; PSALM 45:1–5

*And [Herod] sware unto her, Whatsoever
thou shalt ask of me, I will give it thee,
unto the half of my kingdom.*

MARK 6:23

Here's a foolish promise—one that cost a king his honor and a prophet his life. The king, Herod Antipas, made this offer to his stepdaughter, who had performed a pleasing dance. The girl asked her mother, Herodias, what to request—and the queen, angry at John the Baptist's criticism of her marriage to Herod, demanded the prophet's head. Though few of us have power like Herod, we still need to be careful what we promise. Careless words can create much pain.

Bible reading:

LEVITICUS 25; MARK 6:30–56; PSALM 45:6–12

Thy throne, O God, is for ever and ever:
the sceptre of thy kingdom is a right sceptre.
PSALM 45:6

Disposable products have simplified the lives of millions of people. From razors to forks and diapers to pens, when an object has run its course or usefulness, it's simply discarded and never thought of again. God's rule in the universe is the exact opposite. His throne is forever. It existed before the world came into being and will remain into eternity. Take it as a comfort and a mind boggler, all wrapped in one.

Bible reading:

LEVITICUS 26; MARK 7; PSALM 45:13–17

And [Jesus] said unto her, For this saying go thy way;
the devil is gone out of thy daughter.

MARK 7:29

Jesus' promise to a desperate mother was fulfilled
instantly—and gives us a glimpse into God's heart
for needy people. This non-Jewish woman knew
Jesus could help her demon-possessed daughter,
but Jesus basically said His ministry was only for
the Jews. When the woman responded in humility,
rather than anger, Jesus' heart was moved—and
He gave her exactly what she asked for.

DAY 63

Bible reading:

LEVITICUS 27; MARK 8; PSALM 46

*For whosoever will save his life shall lose it; but
whosoever shall lose his life for my sake and the gospel's,
the same shall save it. For what shall it profit a man,
if he shall gain the whole world, and lose his own soul?*

MARK 8:35–36

❧ ⋆ ❧

You can have everything in this world—wealth,
fame, power—and have nothing. You can have
nothing in this world—no wealth, no fame, no
power—and have everything (Matthew 6:19–21).
God tells us we are not to love the world or anything
of the world (1 John 2:15). We are, instead, to rid
ourselves of worldly things and focus on Christ
and the good news, the only things that matter
now. . .and for eternity.

Bible reading:

NUMBERS 1–2; MARK 9:1–13; PSALM 47

For the LORD most high is terrible; he is a great King over all the earth. . . . For the shields of the earth belong unto God: he is greatly exalted.

PSALM 47:2, 9

It's sometimes hard to think of the whole earth as being a single entity. With wars, feuding factions, and different ideologies, it often seems as though disunity rules the world. But the truth is, there is One who rules over all, whether we all acknowledge His kingship or not. Everything and everyone—from the greatest natural disaster and the most powerful world leader to the smallest grain of sand and lowliest servant—belongs to God.

Bible reading:

*For [Jesus] taught his disciples, and said unto them,
The Son of man is delivered into the hands of men,
and they shall kill him; and after that he is
killed, he shall rise the third day.*

MARK 9:31

Amazing is a good word to describe this promise.
Jesus said He would die and then come back to
life. . .and He did! Many people saw that promise
fulfilled, according to the apostle Paul: Peter, the
twelve disciples, more than five hundred believers
at one time (1 Corinthians 15:5–6). Though we
as Christians can't see Jesus today, we, too, know
He's alive—by the work He does in our hearts.

Bible reading:

NUMBERS 4; MARK 10:1–34; PSALM 48:9–14

And Jesus looking upon them saith, With men it is impossible, but not with God: for with God all things are possible.

MARK 10:27

Throughout our lifetimes, we may be plagued by many troubles. Sickness. Sin. Unemployment. Divorce. Childlessness. The list goes on and on. While we can't rely on people to fix our problems, there is One we can depend on to help get us through when life seems hopeless. God is still in the miracle-working business. Call out to Him today.

Bible reading

NUMBERS 5:1–6:21; MARK 10:35–52;
PSALM 49:1–9

*For even the Son of man came not to be ministered
unto, but to minister, and to give his life
a ransom for many.*

MARK 10:45

Many dignitaries and celebrities are used to being cared for. From an army of servants to outrageous demands at personal appearances, it seems the more money and notoriety a person possesses, the more he or she is pampered. Jesus didn't hold that same notion of entitlement. Not only did He shy away from celebrity, His demonstrated purpose was one of servanthood and care for others.

Bible reading:

NUMBERS 6:22–7:47; MARK 11; PSALM 49:10–20

The LORD lift up his countenance upon thee,
and give thee peace.

NUMBERS 6:26

Here is God's own blessing for His own people—
the ancient Israelites. Aaron the priest was to
say these words over the people, calling down
God's goodness on them. Today, with Jesus as our
High Priest (Hebrews 4:14), we, too, enjoy all the
goodness of God. "To the praise of the glory of
his grace," Paul wrote in Ephesians 1:6, "wherein
he hath made us accepted in the beloved."

Bible reading:

NUMBERS 7:48–8:4; MARK 12:1–27;
PSALM 50:1–15

I know all the fowls of the mountains:
and the wild beasts of the field are mine.

PSALM 50:11

———— ❖ ————

Our God is an all-knowing, all-seeing Creator. Everything in the world was created by Him and is precious to Him. Do you know that He even knows how many hairs you have on your head (Matthew 10:30)? Serving a sovereign Lord should give us confidence to share our faith with others and say with the writer of Hebrews, "I will not fear what man shall do unto me" (Hebrews 13:6).

Bible reading:

NUMBERS 8:5–9:23; MARK 12:28–44;
PSALM 50:16–23

*Whoso offereth praise glorifieth me: and to him
that ordereth his conversation aright
will I shew the salvation of God.*

PSALM 50:23

———

Have you said a prayer of thanks lately? It's easy
to get into the rut of "I need. . . ," "I want. . ."
prayers. But what about those things God has
blessed you with in life? Your family, your friends,
your job, your home. . . God has given you all
these things and more. Be sure to thank Him.
He'll be delighted to hear from you.

Bible reading:

NUMBERS 10–11; MARK 13:1–8; PSALM 51:1–9

Against thee, thee only, have I sinned, and done this evil in thy sight: that thou mightest be justified when thou speakest, and be clear when thou judgest.

PSALM 51:4

It's sometimes difficult for children to accept the direction of a parent—God's children are no exception—but the heavenly Father has parenting figured out. He's always right and always fair. Although His followers may not always understand God's answers or decisions, that doesn't change the fact that He was right yesterday, is right today, and will be right tomorrow.

Bible reading:

Numbers 12–13; Mark 13:9–37; Psalm 51:10–19

And ye shall be hated of all men
for my name's sake.
Mark 13:13

Hold on, now. . .that's not a *nice* promise. Is Jesus really saying that following Him will make people hate us? Well, yes. You don't have to look far to find people who criticize, mock, and slander our Christian faith. But Jesus (a) gave us fair warning, and (b) promises great reward for staying true to Him (Matthew 5:11–12).

Bible reading:

NUMBERS 14; MARK 14:1–31; PSALM 52

The LORD is longsuffering, and of great mercy,
forgiving iniquity and transgression.
NUMBERS 14:18

❖

Ever do something you shouldn't and as a result feel as though you aren't worthy of God's love and mercy? God's love for us never wavers—not even when we're at our worst. What a blessing to know that when we mess up, God will forgive us in an instant. All we need to do is ask (1 John 1:9).

Bible reading:

NUMBERS 15; MARK 14:32–72; PSALM 53

*But he held his peace, and answered nothing. Again the
high priest asked him, and said unto him, Art thou the
Christ, the Son of the Blessed? And Jesus said, I am:
and ye shall see the Son of man sitting on the right hand
of power, and coming in the clouds of heaven.*

MARK 14:61–62

Jesus never denied that He is the Messiah. He
even spent much of His ministry telling and
retelling His followers that He is the Savior of
mankind. Although the statement was powerful
during His ministry, none packed more punch
than standing in front of the high priest and
announcing Himself as the Son of God who will
someday come again.

Bible reading:

NUMBERS 16; MARK 15:1–32; PSALM 54

Behold, God is mine helper:
the Lord is with them that uphold my soul.
PSALM 54:4

Even the richest, strongest, and most intelligent people sometimes need help. The more average among us probably need even more. What better helper than God Himself? The One who created the universe and keeps it running (Colossians 1:16–17), the One who knows everything (Psalm 147:5), the One who loved you enough to send His Son to die on the cross (John 3:16)—He's more than enough for any problem you face!

Bible reading:

Cast thy burden upon the LORD, and he shall sustain thee: he shall never suffer the righteous to be moved.
PSALM 55:22

Life is hard. We come face-to-face with some pretty tough stuff as we journey through the years—difficult relationships, sickness, stress, the death of a loved one—things that leave us feeling weak and hopeless. We don't need to bear these burdens alone. God wants us to give our worries and cares to Him (Matthew 11:28). He'll offer up just the strength we need to make it through.

Bible reading:

NUMBERS 19–20; MARK 16; PSALM 56:1–7

And [the angel] saith unto them, Be not affrighted:
Ye seek Jesus of Nazareth, which was crucified:
he is risen; he is not here: behold the
place where they laid him.

MARK 16:6

Some of Jesus Christ's promises are yet to be fulfilled: His second coming, the completion of heaven. His resurrection, in comparison to some of His other promises, was an instant-gratification kind of promise. Christ's rising from the dead shook His believers and the rest of the world to the core. How much more amazing will His return be?

Bible reading:

Numbers 21:1–22:20; Luke 1:1–25;
Psalm 56:8–13

And the LORD said unto Moses, Make thee a fiery
serpent, and set it upon a pole: and it shall
come to pass, that every one that is bitten,
when he looketh upon it, shall live.

NUMBERS 21:8

The ancient Israelites were in trouble—their complaining had caused God to punish them with poisonous snakes. But when they admitted their sin, God promised a way of escape—and gave a hint of Jesus' perfect sacrifice to come. Like the brass snake, Jesus would be lifted up on a long piece of wood. And by looking to Jesus, we, too, can live.

Bible reading:

NUMBERS 22:21–23:30; LUKE 1:26–56; PSALM 57

And [Balaam] took up his parable, and said, Rise up,
Balak, and hear; hearken unto me, thou son of Zippor:
God is not a man, that he should lie; neither the son
of man, that he should repent: hath he said,
and shall he not do it? or hath he spoken,
and shall he not make it good?

NUMBERS 23:18–19

Often our prayer time can seem so casual that
we imagine God more like a best friend than the
Author of our salvation (Hebrews 12:2). Yet by
His Word the world was made (2 Peter 3:5), and
by His Word we have eternal life (John 6:68).
How comforting to know He has promised that
His Word will never pass away (Matthew 24:35)!

Bible reading:

NUMBERS 24–25; LUKE 1:57–2:20; PSALM 58

*For unto you is born this day in the city of David
a Saviour, which is Christ the Lord.*

LUKE 2:11

No other gift ever given could rival the gift God sent on that Christmas night so long ago. What excitement the shepherds must have felt at hearing the news of Christ's birth from the angels! Because God sent His Son to save us, we are freed from the punishment of sin and death and can have eternal life (John 3:16; 1 John 4:9)—no strings attached. All we need to do is believe and accept this amazing gift.

Bible reading:

NUMBERS 26:1–27:11; LUKE 2:21–38;
PSALM 59:1–8

For mine eyes have seen thy salvation, which thou hast
prepared before the face of all people; a light to lighten
the Gentiles, and the glory of thy people Israel.
LUKE 2:30–32

An inexpensive night-light may save a stubbed toe
or a banged elbow in the darkness. Such a small
and seemingly insignificant source of illumination
means the difference between groggily stumbling
through the unknown and being able to see the
surroundings and maneuver through life. Jesus
was sent to shine on every man, woman, and child
who, otherwise, would flounder in the dark.

Bible reading:

NUMBERS 27:12–29:11; LUKE 2:39–52;
PSALM 59:9–17

The God of my mercy shall prevent me:
God shall let me see my desire upon mine enemies.
PSALM 59:10

From the giant Goliath, to the paranoid King
Saul, to his own ambitious son Absalom, David the
psalm writer had plenty of enemies. But David also
knew he would win in the end. We can claim that
promise too. Our enemies will either pay for their
sins at the final judgment, or (preferably) they'll
join us in the Christian faith. In the meantime,
our job is to love them (Luke 6:27).

Bible reading:

NUMBERS 29:12–30:16; LUKE 3; PSALM 60:1–5

John answered, saying unto them all, I indeed baptize
you with water; but one mightier than I cometh,
the latchet of whose shoes I am not worthy to unloose:
he shall baptize you with the Holy Ghost and with fire.

LUKE 3:16

These words, spoken by John the Baptist, prepared the way for Jesus, as some of the people were questioning and wondering whether John was the promised Savior. Jesus came to earth—fully God and fully man—to teach His followers the way to salvation. Say a prayer of thanks to God today for sending His Son.

Bible reading:

Numbers 31; Luke 4; Psalm 60:6–12

Through God we shall do valiantly:
for he it is that shall tread down our enemies.
Psalm 60:12

Without God's help, humans accomplish nothing. Without God's help, nothing makes sense, and humans have no control over the way the chips fall. With God's help, humans can find meaning, knowing God's in control. Life can be frustrating, confusing, and sometimes scary, but everything is in His hands. Only with God's help can humans make it through life, doing well.

Bible reading:

Numbers 32–33; Luke 5:1–16; Psalm 61

And Jesus said unto Simon, Fear not;
from henceforth thou shalt catch men.
Luke 5:10

For Peter, James, and John, fishing provided a living. . .but Jesus provided a purpose. By changing their job description to "fishers of men," Jesus gave His disciples a task with eternal consequences. As Christians today, we have the same job description. Whether we're nurses or factory workers, salespeople or police officers, president of the United States or a stay-at-home mom, ultimately, we should be "fishers of men."

Bible reading:

NUMBERS 34–36; LUKE 5:17–32; PSALM 62:1–6

My soul, wait thou only upon God;
for my expectation is from him.
PSALM 62:5

God is waiting for you to spend some quiet time with Him. Share what's on your heart—your needs, your hardships, your goals—and wait for Him to respond. Quiet your heart and your mind as you connect with Him. Wait patiently for Him (Psalm 37:7). He is always there to listen and to comfort you—He's the best Friend you could have.

Bible reading:

DEUTERONOMY 1:1–2:25; LUKE 5:33–6:11;
PSALM 62:7–12

Trust in him at all times; ye people, pour out your heart before him: God is a refuge for us. Selah.

PSALM 62:8

As they grow, children find those safety nets—a blanket, a stuffed toy, a thumb to suck—that they need to help avoid the scary parts of life. Similarly, adults trying to avoid the things *they* dread may find themselves in a diversion addiction—movies, food, TV, music; or worse, gambling, drugs, affairs, pornography. God doesn't want His children to rely on such things to soothe the soul. Instead, He offers His arms as a safe haven from the trials life.

*Ye shall not fear them: for the LORD
your God he shall fight for you.*

DEUTERONOMY 3:22

To the ancient Israelites, God was a warrior, fighting for them as they entered the Promised Land. Though 1 John 4:8 tells us "God is love," He still has plenty of fight in Him. God is now directing an invisible war against evil powers, a universal battle that will end when Jesus, the King of kings and Lord of lords, crushes Satan and his followers as described in Revelation 19–20.

Bible reading:

Deuteronomy 4:15–5:22; Luke 6:36–49;
Psalm 63:6–11

*Give, and it shall be given unto you; good measure,
pressed down, and shaken together, and running over,
shall men give into your bosom. For with the same
measure that ye mete withal it shall be
measured to you again.*

Luke 6:38

To all those who have given gifts with the idea of
getting something in return: read Luke 14:12–14.
Jesus said we should invite the least prosperous,
the disabled, and the downtrodden to dinner,
knowing that we'll be rewarded in heaven. God
loves a cheerful giver, and He promises to bless
us when we give to Him (Malachi 3:10).

DEUTERONOMY 5:23–7:26; LUKE 7:1–17;
PSALM 64:1–5

*Know therefore that the LORD thy God, he is God,
the faithful God, which keepeth covenant and
mercy with them that love him and keep his
commandments to a thousand generations.*

DEUTERONOMY 7:9

Promises are made. Promises are broken. We've all
experienced the letdown of a broken promise. It
hurts when you have an expectation, and a friend,
a family member, or a coworker fails to follow
through. What a comfort to know that we have a
Father who keeps *all* His promises, a Friend who
will never let you down—guaranteed.

Bible reading:

DEUTERONOMY 8–9; LUKE 7:18–35; PSALM 64:6–10

And blessed is he,
whosoever shall not be offended in me.
LUKE 7:23

Here's the recipe for a happy life: walk closely with God and be confident in your relationship with Him. Don't worry about the opinions of others who may criticize your Christianity. They'll only steal your joy. Instead, share God's promise of a joyful spirit with others who want to know what's different about your life. They'll be glad you did.

Bible reading:

*And [Jesus] said to the woman,
Thy faith hath saved thee; go in peace.*

LUKE 7:50

Faith is one of those intangible "Christianese" words many believers struggle to wrap their arms around. It's easy to claim faith in an object, idea, or even God, but in Luke 7, it's not the woman's profession of faith that shows her commitment to Christ. In this setting it's her physical acts of humility—washing and drying and putting perfume on Jesus' feet—that are her outward show of faith.

Bible reading:

DEUTERONOMY 12–13; LUKE 8:4–21;
PSALM 65:9–13

*But that on the good ground are they, which in an honest
and good heart, having heard the word, keep it,
and bring forth fruit with patience.*

LUKE 8:15

Jesus' story of seeds and soils describes the different reactions of people who hear God's Word. Some don't respond at all; others show interest but soon fall away. But for those whose hearts are "good ground," there's a wonderful promise: the Word in their lives will bear "fruit," the spiritual fruit that makes our lives full.

Bible reading:

DEUTERONOMY 14:1–16:8; LUKE 8:22–39;
PSALM 66:1–7

*He ruleth by his power for ever; his eyes behold the
nations: let not the rebellious exalt themselves. Selah.*

PSALM 66:7

✦⟶ ✦ ⟵✦

Watch the evening news or read the headlines of
the paper, and you're sure to be depressed about
the state of the world. War. Unrest. Terrorism.
Suffering. Disease. Poverty. We can't possibly
change the entire world through our own actions,
but we can pray for the world. . .and God will
hear us. He alone watches over *all* nations. We can
place the problems of the world in His hands and
know He holds complete control—today and in
the days yet to come.

Bible reading:

DEUTERONOMY 16:9–18:22; LUKE 8:40–56;
PSALM 66:8–15

*That which is altogether just shalt thou follow,
that thou mayest live, and inherit the land
which the LORD thy God giveth thee.*

DEUTERONOMY 16:20

Just as earthly parents have expectations of their children, so, too, does God expect certain things from His children. At the top of that list is a simple idea: "Do what is right." But God doesn't ask His followers to do right for right's sake. His request is to follow what is right, and only what is right—and this will result in an eternal reward.

Bible reading:

*When thou goest out to battle against thine enemies,
and seest horses, and chariots, and a people more than
thou, be not afraid of them: for the LORD thy God is with
thee, which brought thee up out of the land of Egypt.*

DEUTERONOMY 20:1

❧

Here's another promise to ancient Jews that
mirrors God's dealings with Christians today. "I
am with you always," Jesus promised His followers,
"even unto the end of the world" (Matthew 28:20).
If you ever struggle with fear or loneliness, put
bookmarks in your Bible at these two verses!

Bible reading:

DEUTERONOMY 21:10–23:8; LUKE 9:23–42;
PSALM 67

O let the nations be glad and sing for joy:
for thou shalt judge the people righteously,
and govern the nations upon earth. Selah.
PSALM 67:4

We live in an unfair world. Evil sometimes appears to triumph over good, and we're left feeling shortchanged. We can be thankful, though, that the final Judge over all is our merciful Lord—a fair Judge indeed. Praise the Lord for His mercy and truth, which we can always count on in our ever-changing world.

Bible reading:

DEUTERONOMY 23:9–25:19; LUKE 9:43–62;
PSALM 68:1–6

God setteth the solitary in families.
PSALM 68:6

Although God created humans to have fellowship
with one another (Genesis 2:18), the fact remains
that loneliness is real in a world with a population
of more than six billion people. God knew this
would happen. His love offers the shelter and
comfort of home to all who accept it.

Bible reading:

DEUTERONOMY 26:1–28:14; LUKE 10:1–20;
PSALM 68:7–14

---

*And the LORD shall make thee the head, and not the
tail; and thou shalt be above only, and thou shalt not be
beneath; if that thou hearken unto the commandments of
the LORD thy God, which I command thee this day.*

DEUTERONOMY 28:13

Many of God's Old Testament promises were
conditional—*if* the people would do the right
things, *then* God would bless them. Today, though,
in Jesus we receive God's blessing entirely apart
from our own goodness (see Romans 5). We are
truly "above only. . .not. . .beneath," and all
because of God's kindness and love.

*And [Jesus] turned him unto his disciples,
and said privately, Blessed are the eyes
which see the things that ye see.*

LUKE 10:23

So many conundrums consume our days that we
may wonder what it's like to be simply. . .happy.
Jesus wants us to wonder no longer. He wants us to
turn to Him in prayer (Matthew 21:22). He wants
to carry our burdens (Matthew 11:29). He longs to
have us lead lives that are built upon the life-giving
foundation of His Word (John 6:63), and not on
the shifting sands of popular thought.

Bible reading:

DEUTERONOMY 29–30; LUKE 10:38–11:23;
PSALM 68:20–27

*If ye then, being evil, know how to give good gifts unto
your children: how much more shall your heavenly
Father give the Holy Spirit to them that ask him?*

LUKE 11:13

❦

What a beautiful reminder of the Lord's love for us,
His children. While we—imperfect, sinful beings that
we are—strive to give good things to our children,
how does that compare to what God will give to us?
Our God is perfect. Our God is sinless. Our God
is love. Imagine what that means for us if we walk
closely with Him. He will bless us beyond measure
(Luke 11:28).

Bible reading:

*Be strong and of a good courage, fear not, nor be afraid
of them: for the LORD thy God, he it is that doth go
with thee; he will not fail thee, nor forsake thee.*

DEUTERONOMY 31:6

It's human nature to get wrapped up in
relationships—spouses, friends, siblings, parents,
and children. It's also human nature for people
in these relationships to disappoint each other.
But God promises His enduring faithfulness. His
friendship will never disappoint.

Deuteronomy 32:23–33:29; Luke 11:37–54;
Psalm 69:1–9

For their rock is not as our Rock.
Deuteronomy 32:31

Moses likened God to a Rock (notice the capital *R*)—strong, firm, and unchanging. Other religions might have "small-*r* rocks," but they just don't compare to ours. Why not? Because our Rock is the one and only Creator (Genesis 1:1), Sustainer (Romans 11:36), and Savior (Acts 4:11–12). Best of all, He knows everything about us and loves us just the same (Romans 5:8).

Bible reading:

DEUTERONOMY 34–JOSHUA 2; LUKE 12:1–15;
PSALM 69:10–17

---

*Have not I commanded thee? Be strong and of
a good courage; be not afraid, neither be thou
dismayed: for the LORD thy God is with
thee whithersoever thou goest.*

JOSHUA 1:9

Read through today's scripture, and you're
guaranteed to get a courage boost! What a lovely
reminder that even when we are at our weakest,
God is with us. It is through our weakness that
God's power shines through (2 Corinthians 12:9).
The next time you're struggling to get through
a bad day, remember that God is right there,
holding out His arms to you. He'll give you the
comfort and strength you need.

Bible reading:

Joshua 3:1–5:12; Luke 12:16–40; Psalm 69:18–28

*For where your treasure is,
there will your heart be also.*

Luke 12:34

━━━◆━━━

Jesus tells His followers to stop worrying about the details of their lives, to stop saving up earthly riches while ignoring Christ's kingdom. It takes a person with the foresight of heaven to realize the wealth, power, and material things of this world hold no everlasting importance. Jesus promises riches to the heart that makes deposits in heaven.

Bible reading:

JOSHUA 5:13–7:26; LUKE 12:41–48;
PSALM 69:29–36

*I will praise the name of God with a song,
and will magnify him with thanksgiving.*

PSALM 69:30

✦————◆————✦

Here's a promise that we, like the psalm writer,
can make to the Lord. God loves music—especially
when it praises His name. Have you heard a
particular song you can sing to God today? Or
is there one you can compose especially for Him?
Give it a try—when you make God happy, you'll
feel better yourself.

Bible reading:

Joshua 8–9; Luke 12:49–59; Psalm 70

Thou art my help and my deliverer; O Lord.
Psalm 70:5

❧

We all struggle with temptation in one form or another. And it's tough to stand strong all the time. We're only human, after all. When our human weakness threatens to win out, call on the Lord. . .the only One who promises to provide us with a way out when the going gets tough (1 Corinthians 10:13).

Bible reading:

Joshua 10:1–11:15; Luke 13:1–21; Psalm 71:1–6

Then said he, Unto what is the kingdom of God like? and whereunto shall I resemble it? It is like a grain of mustard seed, which a man took, and cast into his garden; and it grew, and waxed a great tree; and the fowls of the air lodged in the branches of it.

Luke 13:18–19

Although Jesus uses the idea of a tiny mustard seed as a metaphor for faith, He also uses this word picture to explain the kingdom of God. His followers may have wondered if Jesus' influence would ever grow beyond the small circle of His disciples. But the Messiah promised God's holy nation will continue to grow until it reaches full maturity.

Bible reading:

JOSHUA 11:16–13:33; LUKE 13:22–35;
PSALM 71:7–16

*And, behold, there are last which shall be first,
and there are first which shall be last.*
LUKE 13:30

God never promised life would be fair. Money,
good looks, and the right connections make life
easy for some people. But that won't always be
the case. Jesus' words give hope that a new day
is coming, when the privileged few aren't always
on top. If you're "last" now, take hope—through
Jesus, you can be first!

Bible reading:

JOSHUA 14–16; LUKE 14:1–15; PSALM 71:17–21

Now therefore give me this mountain,
whereof the LORD spake in that day.

JOSHUA 14:12

Old Caleb was claiming a forty-five-year-old promise: as one of the two faithful spies who argued for taking the Promised Land, Caleb had received God's promise, through Moses, of a choice part of that land. Decades later, he cashed in. Though forty-five years may seem like a long time to us, it's barely a blip on God's eternal radar. Never doubt that He'll make good His promises to you too.

Bible reading:

Joshua 17:1–19:16; Luke 14:16–35;
Psalm 71:22–24

*My lips shall greatly rejoice when I sing unto thee;
and my soul, which thou hast redeemed.*

Psalm 71:23

Has your soul been set free? Or do you feel the weight of a heavy load on your heart? We are able to leave our cares at our Creator's feet (Psalm 55:22), and He promises to relieve us of any burdens we bear. Share your worries and concerns with Him, and feel the weight lift from your soul as it becomes freed from the cares of the world. Then praise God for the good things He has done for you (Isaiah 63:7).

Bible reading:

JOSHUA 19:17–21:42; LUKE 15:1–10;
PSALM 72:1–11

*Likewise, I say unto you, there is joy in the presence
of the angels of God over one sinner that repenteth.*

LUKE 15:10

It's easy to rejoice when good things happen: a
goal achieved, an obstacle overcome, a project
completed. However, when we hear the good
news about a new Christian, the rejoicing isn't
confined to other believers only. The heavens
erupt in beautiful melody and happiness as the
angels celebrate the new reservation for one more
soul in eternity with God.

Bible reading:

Joshua 21:43–22:34; Luke 15:11–32;
Psalm 72:12–20

And he said unto him, Son, thou art ever with me,
and all that I have is thine.

Luke 15:31

Many know the story of the "prodigal son," the runaway who returned home to a loving father's welcome. Less familiar is the story's end, of the prodigal's responsible brother being angered by the father's generosity. The older man's comment, "All that I have is thine," is a picture of God's promise to us as His own heirs (Romans 8:17). Think about that—as Christians, we can enjoy everything God has and is!

Bible reading:

Joshua 23–24; Luke 16:1–18; Psalm 73:1–9

And, behold, this day I am going the way of all the earth:
and ye know in all your hearts and in all your souls, that
not one thing hath failed of all the good things which the
Lord your God spake concerning you; all are come to
pass unto you, and not one thing hath failed thereof.

Joshua 23:14

If God says it, He'll do it. Who else in your life—your friends, your family, your neighbors, your coworkers—can you depend on quite like that? At one time or another, we've all been hurt because of a broken promise. What joy to know that there's One who will always make good on His word. Put your trust in Him today.

Bible reading:

JUDGES 1–2; LUKE 16:19–17:10; PSALM 73:10–20

---

*And the Lord said, If ye had faith as a grain of mustard
seed, ye might say unto this sycamine tree, Be thou
plucked up by the root, and be thou planted
in the sea; and it should obey you.*

LUKE 17:6

Jesus promises great power to His followers who
display only a tiny amount of faith. Faith as small
as a mustard seed, however, isn't the goal. Jesus'
unspoken promise is that a Christian who displays
faith as big as an apple seed or even a peach pit will
be able to do more than move mountains. That
kind of faith can change the world.

Bible reading:

JUDGES 3–4; LUKE 17:11–37; PSALM 73:21–28

*And she said, I will surely go with thee: notwithstanding
the journey that thou takest shall not be for thine honour;
for the LORD shall sell Sisera into the hand of a woman.*

JUDGES 4:9

We can learn a couple of lessons from this promise,
spoken by one woman (Deborah) about another
woman (Jael). First, God knows the future better
than we know the present—because a humble
housewife did indeed kill the mighty warrior
Sisera. Second, though the stories of men tend
to get more ink in the Bible, God also clearly loves
and calls women to accomplish His plans for the
world (see Galatians 3:28).

Bible reading:

JUDGES 5:1–6:24; LUKE 18:1–17; PSALM 74:1–3

*But Jesus called them unto him, and said, Suffer little
children to come unto me, and forbid them not:
for of such is the kingdom of God. Verily I say unto you,
Whosoever shall not receive the kingdom of God as
a little child shall in no wise enter therein.*

LUKE 18:16–17

In the passage above, Jesus is welcoming the little children. He doesn't see their innocence and wonder as an interruption or a nuisance. He reminds His disciples that there is something to be said for a childlike faith with His statement "for of such is the kingdom of God." We don't need to be Bible scholars or experts to inherit the kingdom of God; all we need is childlike faith—pure and simple.

Bible reading:

JUDGES 6:25–7:25; LUKE 18:18–43; PSALM 74:4–11

And the LORD said unto Gideon, By the three hundred men that lapped will I save you, and deliver the Midianites into thine hand.

JUDGES 7:7

What military commander would whittle his force down from thirty-two thousand to three hundred? That's exactly what Gideon did, at God's command. God wanted a small force to fight the Midianites, so the Israelites couldn't say their own strength had achieved the victory. God promised a miracle, and He delivered—when Gideon's tiny band, armed with trumpets and lamps, shocked the sleeping enemy in the dark of night. The Midianites, terrified by the light and sound, attacked each other before other Israelites mopped up the survivors.

Bible reading:

JUDGES 8:1–9:23; LUKE 19:1–28; PSALM 74:12–17

*For the Son of man is come to seek
and to save that which was lost.*

LUKE 19:10

Which is the best promise in the whole Bible? It
might be this one. Jesus came looking for *you*, in
the hope of saving you from the punishment of
sin. And He's perfectly able to do that—you just
have to take hold of the free gift of salvation (see
Romans 3:24). If you haven't taken advantage of
this amazing offer, why not do so now?

Bible reading:

And [Jesus] answered and said unto them,
I tell you that, if these should hold their peace,
the stones would immediately cry out.

LUKE 19:40

Have you heard the expression "Dumb as a box of rocks"? Jesus said that if people didn't praise Him, then the rest of His creation—including stones—would. That's a promise we shouldn't hope to see fulfilled. Don't be dumb—praise the Lord today!

Bible reading:

The earth and all the inhabitants thereof are dissolved:
I bear up the pillars of it. Selah.
PSALM 75:3

God promises to hold the world and its people together when times are unstable. Imagine the entire
earth shaking—creating fear and unease among the
people. Now imagine God's hands wrapped around
the world, holding it steady—and the people sighing
with utter relief. That's what God does. He makes
it possible for us to have calm in a world that is
often filled with chaos and instability.

Bible reading:

For he is not a God of the dead,
but of the living: for all live unto him.
LUKE 20:38

❖────────❖

If some people are guilty of putting God in a box, others are guilty of putting Him in heaven and leaving Him there. God isn't simply sitting on a cloud twiddling His thumbs, waiting for His children to approach the pearly gates. Jesus reminds His followers that His Father is the God of the living. In earthly life and in physical death, He's real and living and vibrant.

Bible reading:

JUDGES 15–16; LUKE 21:1–19; PSALM 76:1–7

*But before all these, they shall lay their hands on you,
and persecute you, delivering you up to the
synagogues, and into prisons, being brought
before kings and rulers for my name's sake.*

LUKE 21:12

❖━━━━❖

Jesus never painted a rosy picture of the Christian life. Hard work, family tensions, and outright persecution might be in line for us, just as they were for the original disciples. But remember this life is short—and, as the apostle Paul promised, "I reckon that the sufferings of this present time are not worthy to be compared with the glory which shall be revealed in us" (Romans 8:18).

Bible reading:

JUDGES 17–18; LUKE 21:20–22:6; PSALM 76:8–12

*And when these things begin to come to pass,
then look up, and lift up your heads; for your
redemption draweth nigh.*

LUKE 21:28

"These things" refers to events that will take place before the return of Christ (see verses 20–27). Terrible things will come to pass. People will fear for their lives; they will be tempted to give up. But the Lord promises that because we have been bought with His blood, we can lift up our heads. Our days of freedom will come—an eternity spent with Him in paradise.

Bible reading:

JUDGES 19:1–20:23; LUKE 22:7–30; PSALM 77:1–11

I cried unto God with my voice, even unto God
with my voice; and he gave ear unto me.

PSALM 77:1

Calling toll-free numbers to most large businesses almost always guarantees the voice on the other end will be an automated service. Making your way through a maze of phone options to a real human is usually frustrating and sometimes impossible. God's hotline guarantees no preprogrammed voice messages. A prayer spoken calmly with hands clasped, or shouted in the middle of a storm, doesn't go unheard. God hears and listens.

JUDGES 20:24–21:25; LUKE 22:31–54;
PSALM 77:12–20

Thou hast with thine arm redeemed thy people,
the sons of Jacob and Joseph. Selah.

PSALM 77:15

This verse tells of God's miraculous deliverance of
the ancient Israelites from their slavery in Egypt.
But God is still in the business of setting people
free today. Here's a promise worth memorizing,
and revisiting day after day: "I am the way, the
truth, and the life" (John 14:6); "ye shall know
the truth, and the truth shall make you free"
(John 8:32).

Bible reading:

Ruth 1–2; Luke 22:55–23:25; Psalm 78:1–4

The LORD recompense thy work, and a full reward
be given thee of the LORD God of Israel,
under whose wings thou art come to trust.

RUTH 2:12

Sing praises to God today for His protection and His strength. In the midst of the storm, He offers us peace (John 14:27). He gives us shelter. He calms our fearful hearts. He wraps us in His love. Nowhere else can we find such comfort. When lightning strikes and winds blow fierce, call out to Him.

Bible reading:

RUTH 3–4; LUKE 23:26–24:12; PSALM 78:5–8

*And as they were afraid, and bowed down their faces
to the earth, they said unto them, Why seek ye the
living among the dead? He is not here, but is risen:
remember how he spake unto you when he was yet
in Galilee, saying, The Son of man must be
delivered into the hands of sinful men,
and be crucified, and the third day rise again.*

LUKE 24:5–7

———✦———

As God's children wait for His promises of heaven
and everlasting life to be fulfilled, it's comforting
to experience promises that have already been
fulfilled. Jesus' biggest promise ever—that He'd
rise from the dead—was fulfilled in a mere three
days, just as He said it would be.

Bible reading:

1 Samuel 1:1–2:21; Luke 24:13–53; Psalm 78:9–16

And she vowed a vow, and said, O Lord of hosts, if thou wilt indeed look on the affliction of thine handmaid, and remember me, and not forget thine handmaid, but wilt give unto thine handmaid a man child, then I will give him unto the Lord all the days of his life.

1 Samuel 1:11

A desperate, childless woman begs for a son, promising to give the boy back in service to God. The Lord blesses Hannah with a son named Samuel, who becomes one of Israel's greatest leaders—but only because Hannah kept her word. As the writer of Ecclesiastes reminds us, "When thou vowest a vow unto God, defer not to pay it; for he hath no pleasure in fools: pay that which thou hast vowed" (Ecclesiastes 5:4).

Bible reading:

1 Samuel 2:22–4:22; John 1:1–28; Psalm 78:17–24

*Wherefore the LORD God of Israel saith. . .
them that honour me I will honour.*

1 Samuel 2:30

Although God was speaking to the high priest Eli concerning his disobedient sons, God's promise applies to us too. "I love them that love me," God says in Proverbs 8:17, "and those that seek me early shall find me." Don't wait another day to honor God; open His Book and spend some time talking to Him. He loves to hear from you!

Bible reading:

1 Samuel 5–7; John 1:29–51; Psalm 78:25–33

And Samuel spake unto all the house of Israel,
saying, If ye do return unto the LORD with all your
hearts, then put away the strange gods and Ashtaroth
from among you, and prepare your hearts unto
the LORD, and serve him only: and he will deliver
you out of the hand of the Philistines.

1 Samuel 7:3

While we might not need to be saved from the
Philistines, this verse is a good reminder that
when we place our faith and trust entirely in the
Lord, He can—and will—do amazing things in our
lives. He will reward those who seek Him with their
whole hearts (Hebrews 11:1, 6). Step out in faith
and be blessed beyond measure today!

Jesus answered and said unto them,
Destroy this temple, and in three days
I will raise it up.

John 2:19

It took more than a lifetime of work for Jesus to change the views held by the religious leaders of His day. His promise was that when His physical body was killed, He'd rise again in three days. The religious leaders of Jesus' time were so focused on the symbolic importance of the actual temple, they completely missed the importance of the temple of God and house for His Spirit, Christ's body.

*Jesus answered and said unto him, Verily, verily,
I say unto thee, Except a man be born again,
he cannot see the kingdom of God.*

John 3:3

Ever hear a kid ask, "Is that a promise or a threat?" These words of Jesus are a bit of both. By being born again, people enter God's kingdom. But there's no entry apart from the free gift of salvation—no amount of kindness, hard work, or charitable giving will punch your ticket to heaven. For more on being "born again," read on to verse 16.

Bible reading:

1 Samuel 12–13; John 3:23–4:10; Psalm 78:56–66

---

*Moreover as for me, God forbid that I should sin
against the Lord in ceasing to pray for you:
but I will teach you the good and the right way.*

1 Samuel 12:23

Near the end of his life, the prophet Samuel
promised the Israelites that he would teach them
"the good and the right way." Verse 24 explains
what that good and right way is: "Fear the Lord,
and serve him in truth with all your heart. . .
consider how great things he hath done for you."
What was good for the ancient Israelites is just as
good for us today.

Bible reading:

1 Samuel 14; John 4:11–38; Psalm 78:67–72

But whosoever drinketh of the water that I shall give him shall never thirst; but the water that I shall give him shall be in him a well of water springing up into everlasting life.

John 4:14

The dry, burning sensation of thirst is one that most humans can easily remedy. The wet refreshment of a tall glass of crystal-clear water sends the most desperate of thirsts away. But it always comes back. Jesus uses an eternal thirst-quenching water as a metaphor for the hope, peace, and satisfaction God offers His children who enter into a relationship with Him. It's water that no amount of Satan-salt can overpower.

Bible reading:

1 Samuel 15–16; John 4:39–54; Psalm 79:1–7

*And Samuel said, Hath the LORD as great delight in
burnt offerings and sacrifices, as in obeying the voice
of the LORD? Behold, to obey is better than sacrifice,
and to hearken than the fat of rams.*

1 Samuel 15:22

Get your arms around this Bible promise, and life
will run much smoother! God wants us to obey
the rules He's set up to protect us and to help us
grow. He's far less interested in our "paying back"
in some way after we've done wrong. What could
we ever pay God anyway? "If a man love me,"
Jesus said, "he will keep my words" (John 14:23).

Bible reading:

1 SAMUEL 17; JOHN 5:1–24; PSALM 79:8–13

Verily, verily, I say unto you, He that heareth my word,
and believeth on him that sent me, hath everlasting
life, and shall not come into condemnation;
but is passed from death unto life.

JOHN 5:24

✦

While it's normal to mourn the passing of loved ones—fellow believers in Christ—isn't it wonderful that we can, at the same time, celebrate their much-anticipated entrance into the presence of God? For those who have trusted in the Lord as their Savior, death isn't the end of life; it's just the beginning of eternity.

Bible reading:

1 SAMUEL 18–19; JOHN 5:25–47; PSALM 80:1–7

*Turn us again, O God of hosts, and cause thy
face to shine; and we shall be saved.*

PSALM 80:7

A person who saves the life of another is often
heralded as a hero. Acts of selflessness, moments
of impulse, and good deeds can result in heroes.
But God's heroic deed of saving His people is a
sacrifice He thoughtfully and consciously made.
The heavenly Father gave up His only Son for
humankind. His powerful grace can save the low
and the mighty.

*And Jonathan said to David, Go in peace, forasmuch
as we have sworn both of us in the name of the LORD,
saying, The LORD be between me and thee,
and between my seed and thy seed for ever.*

1 Samuel 20:42

This promise sealed one of the greatest friendships
of all time. King Saul's son Jonathan, next in line
for the throne, pledged his love and support for
his friend David, chosen by God to be Israel's
next ruler. What a picture of Paul's command to
"in lowliness of mind let each esteem other better
than themselves" (Philippians 2:3)!

Bible reading:

1 Samuel 22–23; John 6:22–42; Psalm 81:1–10

Jesus answered them and said, Verily, verily, I say unto you, Ye seek me, not because ye saw the miracles, but because ye did eat of the loaves, and were filled.

John 6:26

Their physical hunger was only satisfied for a time, and the people went searching for more. Yet Jesus knew their needs went much deeper. Only when we develop a personal relationship with Jesus, and acknowledge Him as Lord and Savior, do we feel truly "filled." Then we can celebrate the promise along with the psalmist: "O taste and see that the LORD is good" (Psalm 34:8).

1 SAMUEL 24:1–25:31; JOHN 6:43–71;
PSALM 81:11–16

Oh that my people had hearkened unto me,
and Israel had walked in my ways! I should soon
have subdued their enemies, and turned my
hand against their adversaries.

PSALM 81:13–14

Do you ever long for strength and courage in
the face of your enemies? Look to this promise
when you're feeling weak and helpless. The Lord
offers His power to help us defeat those who rise
against us—if only we listen to Him and obey Him.
He will never leave us to fight our battles alone
(Hebrews 13:5–6).

Bible reading:

1 Samuel 25:32–27:12; John 7:1–24; Psalm 82

Arise, O God, judge the earth:
for thou shalt inherit all nations.

Psalm 82:8

❖

National borders, cultural differences, and racial friction are just a few of the issues that plague humankind's desire for unity. Finding common ground is often difficult if not impossible. No matter how vast the canyon between the nations of the world, the truth is that God is the Creator of all. His children can find unity in Him.

DAY 143

Bible reading:

1 Samuel 28–29; John 7:25–8:11; Psalm 83

Jesus stood and cried, saying, If any man thirst,
let him come unto me, and drink.

John 7:37

What's better than a cool glass of water on a hot, dry day? Jesus paints that picture of Himself, promising spiritual refreshment to anyone who turns to Him in faith. The thirsty soul and others around benefit, for "he that believeth on me, as the scripture hath said, out of his belly shall flow rivers of living water" (John 7:38). Don't you want to be refreshed? Don't you want to be a refresher?

Bible reading:

1 Samuel 30–31; John 8:12–47; Psalm 84:1–4

Blessed are they that dwell in thy house:
they will be still praising thee. Selah.

Psalm 84:4

Some Christians radiate joy wherever they go. They can't help but pass their happiness on to others—through a smile, a kind word, a helping hand. As a child of God, this same kind of joy belongs to you too. Let your heart fill with joy (Psalm 28:7), but don't keep it to yourself. Pass it on!

Bible reading:

2 SAMUEL 1–2; JOHN 8:48–9:12; PSALM 84:5–12

Jesus said unto them, Verily, verily,
I say unto you, Before Abraham was, I am.
JOHN 8:58

Christians tend to think of eternity in terms of
the future: heaven will be the eternal home for
God's children. Eternity, however, stretches not
only into the future but into the past as well.
Jesus told His followers that He was and is and
always will be. Christ promises His children this
everlasting comfort of His presence.

DAY 146

Bible reading:

2 SAMUEL 3–4; JOHN 9:13–34; PSALM 85:1–7

Thou hast forgiven the iniquity of thy people,
thou hast covered all their sin. Selah.

PSALM 85:2

Living as we do in the "Christian era," we can read
Psalm 85:2 in light of Jesus' perfect sacrifice. His
death on the cross covered every sin, paving the
way for the forgiveness of everyone who asks. God
takes His promise of forgiveness *very* seriously—it
cost Him the death of His Son!

Bible reading:

2 SAMUEL 5:1–7:17; JOHN 9:35–10:10;
PSALM 85:8–13

Yea, the LORD shall give that which is good;
and our land shall yield her increase.

PSALM 85:12

We've all heard the saying "Good things come to those who wait." But let's improve upon that statement with "Good things come to those who put their trust in the Lord." It's not about waiting it out—something good eventually has to happen to us, right? But it is about loving the Lord and trusting Him to give us exactly what we need.

Bible reading:

2 Samuel 7:18–10:19; John 10:11–30;
Psalm 86:1–10

*And I give unto [my sheep] eternal life;
and they shall never perish, neither shall any
man pluck them out of my hand.*

John 10:28

Jesus' followers would have been very familiar with the relationship between a shepherd and his sheep. As a shepherd cares for his flock and looks out for its well-being, so much more does Jesus value each of His followers. Jesus is the ultimate Shepherd as He extends eternal life, freedom from punishment, and safety in His hand.

Bible reading:

2 Samuel 11:1–12:25; John 10:31–11:16;
Psalm 86:11–17

*When Jesus heard that, he said, This sickness is not
unto death, but for the glory of God, that the Son
of God might be glorified thereby.*

John 11:4

Nobody asks for illness or injury. But God has promised that even our worst experiences can serve His good purposes. Remember Romans 8:28? "And we know that all things work together for good to them that love God, to them who are the called according to his purpose." Having a tough day (or week, or year, or life)? You can still bring honor to God.

DAY 150

Bible reading:

2 Samuel 12:26–13:39; John 11:17–54; Psalm 87

*Jesus said unto her, I am the resurrection,
and the life: he that believeth in me,
though he were dead, yet shall he live.*

JOHN 11:25

Martha's brother Lazarus had been in his tomb for four days when Jesus arrived to speak these words. Why had Jesus waited so long to come to the aid of His dear friend? The answer is clear: to demonstrate in no uncertain terms that He is God. The One who gives life can be no other than the One who created the heavens and the earth from nothing (see Genesis 1:1).

Bible reading:

2 Samuel 14:1–15:12; John 11:55–12:19;
Psalm 88:1–9

Let my prayer come before thee:
incline thine ear unto my cry.
Psalm 88:2

Although the Lord may not seem to hear us when we call out to Him, we must persevere. Luke 18:1 reminds us that we should pray and never give up. Just because we haven't received an answer doesn't mean we should quit praying about a particular matter; it simply means we should keep praying, with faith in our hearts, that the Lord will come through—at just the right time.

Bible reading:

2 Samuel 15:13–16:23; John 12:20–43;
Psalm 88:10–18

*If any man serve me, let him follow me;
and where I am, there shall also my servant be:
if any man serve me, him will my Father honour.*

John 12:26

It isn't often that we hear the word *honor* uttered in a sentence. When we do, the term seems rather outdated—a thing of the past. But Jesus says if we serve Him, His Father will honor us. He will treat us with high regard. While the people we live and work among may not accept our service to the Lord with open hearts and minds, we need to look at the bigger picture and relish the thought that our Father in heaven will reward us for our endeavors. And that's all that really matters anyway.

Bible reading:

2 Samuel 17:1–18:18; John 12:44–13:20;
Psalm 89:1–6

I am come a light into the world, that whosoever
believeth on me should not abide in darkness.

John 12:46

———————

Fear of darkness is one of those childhood phobias
that sometimes stick around to adulthood. Why?
Because we can't see in the dark. Darkness can lead
to uncertainty, confusion, and even paranoia. Evil
creatures lurk in the dark. Secrets hide in the dark.
Jesus offered an alternative to the darkness and
evil of the world when He promised to illuminate
the lives of His children who trust in Him.

Bible reading:

2 Samuel 18:19–19:39; John 13:21–38;
Psalm 89:7–13

---

*O Lord God of hosts, who is a strong Lord like unto
thee? or to thy faithfulness round about thee?*

Psalm 89:8

The word *faithful* can be defined as "firm in
adherence to promises." And that describes God
exactly. Through almost half a year now, you've read
promises from scripture and seen how the Lord has
fulfilled every one. Say today with the psalm writer,
"All around You we see how faithful You are!"

Bible reading:

2 Samuel 19:40–21:22; John 14:1–17;
Psalm 89:14–18

---

*Jesus saith unto him, I am the way, the truth,
and the life: no man cometh unto the Father, but by me.*
John 14:6

Good works won't get you there. Being nice won't get you there. Success won't get you there. Lots of money won't get you there. The only way there—to eternal life in heaven with our Creator—is through Jesus (Ephesians 2:8–9). If we believe in Him and accept His gift of salvation, we will one day live in a state of perfect peace and joy in a place prepared especially for us, His children (John 14:2–3).

Bible reading:

2 Samuel 22:1–23:7; John 14:18–15:27;
Psalm 89:19–29

*But the Comforter, which is the Holy Ghost, whom
the Father will send in my name, he shall teach you
all things, and bring all things to your remembrance,
whatsoever I have said unto you.*

John 14:26

When Jesus took up residence with His Father in
heaven, His followers may have felt ill equipped
to continue growing His kingdom on earth.
Thankfully, the Messiah didn't leave them empty
handed. He extends that same help to every
Christian: the Holy Spirit, who fills in the gaps
when head knowledge fails.

Bible reading:

2 Samuel 23:8–24:25; John 16:1–22;
Psalm 89:30–37

Ye shall be sorrowful,
but your sorrow shall be turned into joy.

John 16:20

Jesus made this promise to His disciples as He described his impending death and resurrection. But the idea of Jesus' words applies to us today: We have sorrow and trouble in this world (John 16:33), but look forward to a day when every tear will be wiped away by God Himself (Revelation 7:17). No matter how hard this world may be, a better day is coming!

Bible reading:

1 Kings 1; John 16:23–17:5; Psalm 89:38–52

Then Adonijah the son of Haggith exalted himself,
saying, I will be king.
1 Kings 1:5

Adonijah, a son of King David, promised himself
and his followers that he would follow his father
on the throne. But David had said his younger
son Solomon would be king—so Adonijah's words
proved empty. Some "promises" are beyond our
ability to keep, and shouldn't even be made.
"There are many devices in a man's heart;
nevertheless the counsel of the LORD, that shall
stand" (Proverbs 19:21).

Bible reading:

1 KINGS 2; JOHN 17:6–26; PSALM 90:1–12

Holy Father, keep through thine own name those whom
thou hast given me, that they may be one, as we are.
JOHN 17:11

Jesus prayed this prayer just before the arrest that led to His crucifixion. Even while He was anticipating the horrible pain that awaited Him in the coming hours, the Messiah spent time praying for Christians. He promises unity among believers who tap into the power of the name of God.

Bible reading:

That the saying might be fulfilled, which he spake,
Of them which thou gavest me have I lost none.

John 18:9

When we come to God through Jesus, we're secure. God has wrapped His protective wings around us (Psalm 63:7), He is a Strong Tower for us (Proverbs 18:10), and He cares for us (1 Peter 5:7). Jesus has said that nobody will snatch us from His hands (John 10:28). Come to God through Jesus, and He'll never let you go.

Bible reading:

1 Kings 5–6; John 18:28–19:5; Psalm 91:1–10

And the LORD gave Solomon wisdom,
as he promised him.
1 Kings 5:12

❖━━━━━◦❖◦━━━━━❖

Solomon once wrote, "How much better is it to get wisdom than gold!" (Proverbs 16:16), but as one who abused that gift, he also knew the flip side of such power (Ecclesiastes 1:18). Far better, then, to be filled, as Paul writes, "with the knowledge of his will in all wisdom and spiritual understanding" (Colossians 1:9). When we seek God's will and wisdom, we can live lives that are "worthy of the Lord unto all pleasing" (Colossians 1:10).

Bible reading:

1 Kings 7; John 19:6–24; Psalm 91:11–16

For he shall give his angels charge over thee,
to keep thee in all thy ways.

Psalm 91:11

No need for armed bodyguards. No need to let fear overtake us. No need to cower in the face of our enemies. God is our Protector. His strength and power will keep us from harm. His shelter is enough to keep us safe. If we place our hope and trust in Him, He'll even command His angels to care for us. Nowhere else but God's Word can you find a promise like that.

Bible reading:

1 Kings 8:1–53; John 19:25–42; Psalm 92:1–9

After this, Jesus knowing that all things were now accomplished, that the scripture might be fulfilled.

John 19:28

Jesus Christ fulfilled more than three hundred Old Testament prophesies about the Messiah. From the ministry of John the Baptist (Isaiah 40:3) and Jesus' birth in Bethlehem (Micah 5:2), to His betrayal by a friend (Psalm 41:9) and the piercing of His hands and feet (Psalm 22:16), Jesus' life had been spelled out in prophecy generations before He stepped foot on earth. He is truly a promise fulfilled.

*To shew that the LORD is upright: he is my rock,
and there is no unrighteousness in him.*

PSALM 92:15

Bottom line: you can trust God. He is faithful.
He's a Rock. He's absolutely right and good in
every way. Even when you're going through hard
times. Even when life isn't making sense. Even
when God seems distant. Think about all the
fulfilled promises you've read about through
the first five and a half months of this year—and
recommit yourself to the good and faithful God
who loves you!

Bible reading:

1 Kings 10:14–11:43; John 20:19–31; Psalm 93

Jesus saith unto him, Thomas, because thou hast seen me, thou hast believed: blessed are they that have not seen, and yet have believed.

John 20:29

Are you a Doubting Thomas? Do you need to see something in order to believe it? Or are you a Believing Benjamin—believing without needing visual evidence? The Lord wants us to have faith in His promises without a need for signs or proof to back them up. If we have faith—placing our trust in His Word—He promises our happiness, pure and simple.

Bible reading:

1 Kings 12:1–13:10; John 21; Psalm 94:1–11

The LORD knoweth the thoughts of man,
that they are vanity.

PSALM 94:11

Sometimes it's difficult to get past daily stresses to see what's really important. When everything seems hopeless, helpless, and out of control, God still sees the big picture. His children can take comfort in the fact that God knows all and sees all. And His shoulders are strong enough to bear the stresses and frustrations of the day.

Bible reading:

1 KINGS 13:11–14:31; ACTS 1:1–11;
PSALM 94:12–23

*But ye shall receive power, after that the Holy Ghost
is come upon you: and ye shall be witnesses unto me
both in Jerusalem, and in all Judaea, and in Samaria,
and unto the uttermost part of the earth.*

ACTS 1:8

Though the resurrected Jesus had to leave earth for
heaven, He promised to send His Holy Spirit to His
followers. And what a powerful presence the Spirit is!
Read the book of Acts to see what the Spirit helped
the early Christians do. Read Galatians 5:22–23 to
see what He'll help you to achieve. Don't miss out
on this promise!

1 Kings 15:1–16:20; Acts 1:12–26; Psalm 95

In his hand are the deep places of the earth:
the strength of the hills is his also. The sea is his,
and he made it: and his hands formed the dry land.

Psalm 95:4–5

Take a good look at all our Creator has provided for our enjoyment—the mountains, the sea, the sky, the flowers and trees. All these beautiful things were created with us in mind. . .and all belong to Him. Thank the Lord today for His goodness and for the simple pleasures He has placed in your backyard.

Bible reading:

1 Kings 16:21–18:19; Acts 2:1–21; Psalm 96:1–8

For all the gods of the nations are idols: but the Lord made the heavens. Honour and majesty are before him: strength and beauty are in his sanctuary.

Psalm 96:5–6

Fans of professional athletes and teams often find themselves defending the greatness of their heroes. It's a "my dad is stronger than your dad" kind of argument that will never really be resolved. Children of God sometimes find themselves defending their Father to a world that thinks truth is relative. But all other gods—wealth, power, possessions—are empty, and only the true Creator can claim great power.

*Yet I have left me seven thousand in Israel,
all the knees which have not bowed unto Baal,
and every mouth which hath not kissed him.*

1 KINGS 19:18

Poor Elijah was depressed. Soon after destroying the prophets of Baal at Carmel, he heard Queen Jezebel's threat to snuff out *his* life—and, thinking he was the only true prophet left, Elijah lost heart. But God promised to keep a small army of faithful people in Israel—just as He keeps His program alive today. Sure, you're living in a dark, scary world. But remember that He'll never leave you alone (see Matthew 19:29).

Bible reading:

1 KINGS 20; ACTS 2:42–3:26; PSALM 97:1–6

Clouds and darkness are round about him:
righteousness and judgment are the
habitation of his throne.

PSALM 97:2

When you quarrel with your spouse, your kids
won't listen to you, and your boss is on the verge
of handing you a pink slip, there's a tendency to
blame God for your misfortune. Still, we need to
remember that our heavenly Father is always just.
He causes His sun to rise over all people. . .and
His rain to pour down as well (Matthew 5:45).

Ye that love the LORD, hate evil: he preserveth
the souls of his saints; he delivereth them
out of the hand of the wicked.

PSALM 97:10

Perfect peace is the gift we will receive if we remain faithful to our Father God (John 14:27). With Him as our closest companion, we can weather any storm. The world may toss some scary things our way, but we can stand untouched with God as our Shield. In the words of Jesus, "These things I have spoken unto you, that in me ye might have peace. In the world ye shall have tribulation: but be of good cheer; I have overcome the world" (John 16:33).

Bible reading:

1 Kings 22:29–2 Kings 1; Acts 4:23–5:11;
Psalm 98

All the ends of the earth have seen
the salvation of our God.
Psalm 98:3

An open eye and a listening ear can see and hear God's graces on a daily basis: a helping hand from a coworker on the busiest of days; a series of green traffic lights to get to an appointment on time. That same sensitivity to God can see His saving power on a grander scale: a hurricane heading straight for land veers out to sea; a biopsy expected to indicate cancer comes back cancer-free. Everyone everywhere has experienced this saving power. It's up to His children to help others see it.

Bible reading

2 KINGS 2–3; ACTS 5:12–28; PSALM 99

And Elisha said unto him, As the LORD liveth,
and as thy soul liveth, I will not leave thee.
2 KINGS 2:2

❖━━━━●❖●━━━━❖

This promise is loyalty on display: Elisha, successor
to the prophet Elijah, refused to leave his mentor's
side until God Himself swept Elijah up to heaven in
a chariot of fire. How much better would our world
be if everyone kept promises as well as Elisha did?

Bible reading:

2 Kings 4; Acts 5:29–6:15; Psalm 100

For the LORD is good; his mercy is everlasting;
and his truth endureth to all generations.

Psalm 100:5

You can leave material goods. . . . You can leave money. . . . You can leave a name. . . . But the loving-kindness of the Lord. . .what a legacy to hand down to our children. And He promises just that for our children to come. We can leave a lasting inheritance for future generations—one that won't rust or fade over time. One that will never be depleted—because the Lord has promised it will last forever.

Bible reading:

2 Kings 5:1–6:23; Acts 7:1–16; Psalm 101

I will sing of mercy and judgment:
unto thee, O Lord, will I sing.

Psalm 101:1

We learn at an early age that life isn't always fair. At work, the immoral succeed and the cheaters get the promotion. In the court system, criminals go free and victims suffer again and again. But God doesn't play by the rules of the world. His righteous fairness transcends the imperfection of the world. He's truly worthy of our praise!

Bible reading:

And he said, Behold, thou shalt see it with
thine eyes, but shalt not eat thereof.

2 Kings 7:2

❖————◦————❖

Samaria was under military siege—and starving.
When the prophet Elisha told the city's leaders
that God was about to end the famine, one
military captain doubted. Elisha's response was
a frightening promise—proven true the next
day when crowds rushing for a miraculous food
supply trampled the captain to death. The point?
Never doubt God's word or abilities. Take what
He offers, with gratitude.

Bible reading:

2 Kings 8:16–9:37; Acts 7:37–53;
Psalm 102:8–17

He will regard the prayer of the destitute,
and not despise their prayer.

Psalm 102:17

When you're in need, sometimes you feel utterly helpless and alone. Your closest friends may desert you. Your family may fail to give you support and help when you need it most. But there is One who will never turn His back on you. Draw near to Him and share your deepest needs and hurts with Him. You'll be glad you did.

Bible reading:

2 KINGS 10–11; ACTS 7:54–8:8; PSALM 102:18–28

But thou art the same,
and thy years shall have no end.
PSALM 102:27

High school reunions bring their fair share of jitters to many classmates who haven't seen each other in years. Who has changed the most? Who looks the same? Who is the unexpected success story, and who is falling short of his or her potential? God is different from long-lost classmates. No matter how long one of God's children strays from a relationship with Him, the Father will be the same loving, powerful Creator that He has been forever.

---

2 KINGS 12–13; ACTS 8:9–40; PSALM 103:1–9

The LORD is merciful and gracious,
slow to anger, and plenteous in mercy.

PSALM 103:8

How much "loving-pity and kindness" does God
have toward us? Enough to send His only Son,
Jesus, to die on the cross for us—even while we
were still sinners (Romans 5:8). Enough to show
patience to all people, not wanting anyone to miss
the blessings of heaven (2 Peter 3:9). Enough to
fulfill every promise He makes to us.

Bible reading:

2 KINGS 14–15; ACTS 9:1–16; PSALM 103:10–14

*But the Lord said unto him, Go thy way: for he is
a chosen vessel unto me, to bear my name before the
Gentiles, and kings, and the children of Israel.*

ACTS 9:15

When the Lord gave this order to Ananias, the godly
man was naturally skeptical. How could God have
chosen Saul of Tarsus, a known killer of Christians,
to be His missionary? Yet the man who would be
called Paul became one of the most zealous evangelists
of all time. How does God choose anyone? Let's
remember God's promise to Samuel: "The LORD
looketh on the heart" (1 Samuel 16:7).

Bible reading:

2 KINGS 16–17; ACTS 9:17–31; PSALM 103:15–22

The LORD hath prepared his throne in the heavens;
and his kingdom ruleth over all.

PSALM 103:19

❖━━━━━━❖

Presidents. . .senators. . .civic officials. . . No matter who they are or what the issue, our leaders have drastically different viewpoints. Sometimes they make bad decisions. No matter who holds an office, we're sure to be disappointed in a leader at some point. What a joy to know that while our earthly rulers may fail, we can always rely on our King in heaven to retain complete control over all.

Bible reading:

2 KINGS 18:1–19:7; ACTS 9:32–10:16;
PSALM 104:1–9

---

*[God,] who coverest thyself with light as with a garment:
who stretchest out the heavens like a curtain: who layeth
the beams of his chambers in the waters: who maketh
the clouds his chariot: who walketh upon the wings
of the wind: Who maketh his angels spirits;
his ministers a flaming fire.*

PSALM 104:2–4

God is in control. It's a simple fact, but in it
are wrapped details that are easy to overlook.
He controls all aspects of the world, from light
and clouds to water and wind. His influence
spreads over everything humans understand and
everything beyond our grasp. He's in charge, and
that's something we can rely on.

Bible reading:

2 Kings 19:8–20:21; Acts 10:17–33;
Psalm 104:10–23

*Now therefore are we all here present before God,
to hear all things that are commanded thee of God.*

Acts 10:33

When the Roman soldier Cornelius made this promise to the apostle Peter, God revealed that His plan of salvation was for *everyone*—not only Jews. Cornelius and his family believed in Jesus and received the Holy Spirit, and the world has never been the same. Just think how your own life might change if you sincerely repeated the promise of Cornelius.

Bible reading:

2 Kings 21:1–22:20; Acts 10:34–11:18;
Psalm 104:24–30

*Whosoever believeth in him shall
receive remission of sins.*
Acts 10:43

❖——◆——❖

Guilt. We've all experienced it at some point in
our lives. A "little white lie" here. A bit of gossip
passed along there. That really big, super-duper
sin we've kept hidden from everyone. You get the
picture. While others may not be aware of our
shortcomings, God knows about them all. We
can't keep anything from Him. The good news is
that all we need to do is ask Him for forgiveness,
and it's done—immediately, right then and there
(1 John 1:9).

Bible reading:

2 KINGS 23; ACTS 11:19–12:17; PSALM 104:31–35

He looketh on the earth, and it trembleth:
he toucheth the hills, and they smoke.

PSALM 104:32

God is love, but God is also mighty power. The same God who extends grace to all who accept it also holds the power to destroy those who anger Him. For a Christian, the Creator's power can be a source of comfort as well as fear. It's only through the soul-cleansing blood of Christ that Christians can be confident in the fact that God's power is there to provide protection.

Bible reading:

2 KINGS 24–25; ACTS 12:18–13:13; PSALM 105:1–7

*And the LORD sent against him bands of the Chaldees,
and bands of the Syrians, and bands of the Moabites,
and bands of the children of Ammon, and sent them
against Judah to destroy it, according to the word of the
LORD, which he spake by his servants the prophets.*

2 KINGS 24:2

❖━━❖━━❖

Some of the Bible's promises aren't pleasant—
they're warnings of punishment and destruction
and pain. But notice how often God provides
an "out" from His anger. All through the Old
Testament, He said things like, "If you obey,
you'll be safe." In the New Testament, God offers
Jesus Christ as our escape from punishment and
pain. Have you grabbed hold of that promise in
John 3:16?

Bible reading:

1 CHRONICLES 1–2; ACTS 13:14–43;
PSALM 105:8–15

He hath remembered his covenant for ever, the word
which he commanded to a thousand generations.

PSALM 105:8

Have you ever made a promise and soon forgot about it? "I promise I'll call you tonight at 7:00." "I promise I'll be there!" "I promise I'll. . ." We don't always place a lot of value on the promises we make to others, but there is One who stays true to His word—no matter how big or small the promise. Praise Him today.

Bible reading:

1 Chronicles 3:1–5:10; Acts 13:44–14:10;
Psalm 105:16–28

---

*For so hath the Lord commanded us, saying, I have set
thee to be a light of the Gentiles, that thou shouldest
be for salvation unto the ends of the earth.*

Acts 13:47

Paul and Barnabas are quoting a passage from
Isaiah 49, explaining to Jewish leaders that
the Word of God is extended to every person,
regardless of race, family lineage, social status,
or location. This promise reaches to the twenty-
first century, as Christians are commanded in
the Great Commission to share this promise of
salvation from punishment with the entire world.

Bible reading:

1 CHRONICLES 5:11–6:81; ACTS 14:11–28;
PSALM 105:29–36

*Confirming the souls of the disciples, and exhorting them
to continue in the faith, and that we must through
much tribulation enter into the kingdom of God.*

ACTS 14:22

Oh, no. . .another promise of trials in the
Christian life! This time, the apostle Paul makes
the promise, and he knows what he's saying: just
three verses earlier, he was stoned and left for
dead by an angry mob in Lycaonia. Though it may
not seem fair, God says we'll sometimes suffer for
following Him. But He also promises blessing
amid the pain (see Matthew 5:11–12).

Bible reading:

1 CHRONICLES 7:1–9:9; ACTS 15:1–18;
PSALM 105:37–45

*Known unto God are all his works
from the beginning of the world.*
ACTS 15:18

From the first words of the Old Testament—that God created heaven and earth—to the last—that Jesus will someday come to earth again—God has mapped out His plan for the world. And while we don't know the exact day or time of His return (Matthew 24:36), we can put our faith in the One called Alpha and Omega (Revelation 22:13), the First and the Last, and in His promises.

DAY 192

Bible reading.

1 CHRONICLES 9:10–11:9; ACTS 15:19–41;
PSALM 106:1–12

Praise ye the LORD. O give thanks unto the LORD;
for he is good: for his mercy endureth for ever.
PSALM 106:1

Perfect weather on your day off. A warm house on a cold day. A much-needed hug from a friend. A pay increase at just the right time. It's not often that we stop and take notice of the little things the Lord has done for us. But each day, you're sure to find one thing to be thankful for. What will you praise Him for today?

1 Chronicles 11:10–12:40; Acts 16:1–15;
Psalm 106:13–27

For at that time day by day there came to David to help
him, until it was a great host, like the host of God.
1 Chronicles 12:22

During times of war, we hear news about troop
deployment and reinforcement, phrases that
sometimes give the idea that our side isn't exactly
winning. God's army isn't like human armies;
His troop levels are big enough to conquer any
enemy—even Satan himself.

Bible reading:

1 Chronicles 13–15; Acts 16:16–40;
Psalm 106:28–33

And they said, Believe on the Lord Jesus Christ,
and thou shalt be saved, and thy house.

Acts 16:31

These seventeen words encapsulate the message
of the entire Bible. In eternity past, long before
Adam and Eve's sin in the Garden of Eden, God
had planned a way to save people from punishment
(Ephesians 1:3–5). In eternity future, we'll enjoy
the pleasures and benefits of heaven (Psalm 16:11).
And it's all through our faith in Jesus Christ.

Bible reading:

1 Chronicles 16–17; Acts 17:1–14;
Psalm 106:34–43

Seek the LORD and his strength,
seek his face continually.
1 Chronicles 16:11

❖

What do you do to rejuvenate when you're feeling weak? Take a long nap? Devour a home-cooked meal? Take a brisk walk? What about asking the Lord to give you strength? He alone has just the grace we need during our weakest moments (2 Corinthians 12:9). Ask Him to infuse you with His power. You won't regret it!

Bible reading:

1 Chronicles 18–20; Acts 17:15–34;
Psalm 106:44–48

*God that made the world and all things therein, seeing
that he is Lord of heaven and earth, dwelleth not in
temples made with hands; neither is worshipped with
men's hands, as though he needed any thing, seeing he
giveth to all life, and breath, and all things.*

Acts 17:24–25

Evidence of god and goddess worship pervaded
every aspect of life in first-century Athens, from
worship to pampering the gods by supplying them
with favorite food and material objects. Paul, in
his speech on Mars Hill, introduced the true God
who is self-sufficient and doesn't rely on humans
to meet His needs. Now, this is the God who truly
deserves our worship!

For he satisfieth the longing soul,
and filleth the hungry soul with goodness.
PSALM 107:9

This promise of the Psalms was echoed in Jesus' Sermon on the Mount, when the Lord taught, "Blessed are they which do hunger and thirst after righteousness: for they shall be filled" (Matthew 5:6). Filled with what? Good things like the spiritual fruit of Galatians 5:22–23: love, joy, peace, longsuffering, gentleness, goodness, faith, meekness, and temperance.

Bible reading:

1 Chronicles 23–25; Acts 18:24–19:10;
Psalm 107:10–16

*Then they cried unto the Lord in their trouble,
and he saved them out of their distresses. He brought
them out of darkness and the shadow of death,
and brake their bands in sunder.*

Psalm 107:13–14

Pride sometimes keeps us from asking for help. Deep down we know we just can't get through tough times on our own, but we try anyway. . .and ultimately fail. God didn't create us to be self-sufficient loners. He created us for relationship—most importantly, a relationship with Him. Reach out to Him with your troubled heart and pour out your burdens to Him (Matthew 11:28). He'll lift you out of the darkness and into the light.

Bible reading:

1 CHRONICLES 26–27; ACTS 19:11–22;
PSALM 107:17–32

*Then they cry unto the LORD in their trouble,
and he bringeth them out of their distresses.
He maketh the storm a calm, so that the
waves thereof are still.*

PSALM 107:28–29

Storms of troubles come in every life—from physical illness and relationship issues to financial woes and persecution. God promises to hear us when His children call out to Him. He sees the big picture, sometimes quieting the storm and sometimes helping us grow in the situation. Either way, He offers inner peace.

Bible reading:

1 Chronicles 28–29; Acts 19:23–41;
Psalm 107:33–38

*And thou, Solomon my son, know thou the God of thy
father, and serve him with a perfect heart and with
a willing mind: for the LORD searcheth all hearts,
and understandeth all the imaginations of the thoughts:
if thou seek him, he will be found of thee.*

1 Chronicles 28:9

Because He is so different from us, God is mysterious.
How can we possibly understand an eternal, all-
powerful, all-knowing Being? And yet, God has
promised that when we seek Him with all our heart,
we'll find Him (Jeremiah 29:13). . .and not only
find Him, but *know* Him (Jeremiah 24:7). God is
never far away—He's as close as your next thought.

Bible reading:

2 CHRONICLES 1–3; ACTS 20:1–16;
PSALM 107:39–43

*Yet setteth he the poor on high from affliction, and
maketh him families like a flock. . . . Whoso is wise,
and will observe these things, even they shall
understand the lovingkindness of the LORD.*

PSALM 107:41, 43

God usually hears from us when we're in crisis
mode. We've tried everything else and turn to
Him as a last resort. Yet His heart is filled with
compassion for His children, and time after time,
He responds to our cries for help with answers
that are more satisfying than we could imagine. As
Jeremiah writes, "It is of the LORD's mercies that
we are not consumed, because his compassions
fail not. They are new every morning: great is thy
faithfulness" (Lamentations 3:22–23).

Bible reading

2 Chronicles 4:1–6:11; Acts 20:17–38;
Psalm 108

*Through God we shall do valiantly: for he it is
that shall tread down our enemies.*

Psalm 108:13

Want to change the world? Partner up with God, and see what amazing things you can do together. With God at your side—guiding you, loving you, blessing you—there's no limit to what you can accomplish (Mark 9:23). Step out in faith, and ask God to work through you. Then wait and see what happens next. Enjoy the ride!

O LORD God of Israel, there is no God like thee in the heaven, nor in the earth; which keepest covenant.

2 CHRONICLES 6:14

Here's a promise applicable to every other Bible promise: God keeps His promises! Human promises fail, deals fall through, people will let you down, but God's promises come with an eternal warranty. Invest in Him for guaranteed returns.

Bible reading:

2 Chronicles 7:11–9:28; Acts 21:15–32;
Psalm 109:21–31

*For he shall stand at the right hand of the poor,
to save him from those that condemn his soul.*

Psalm 109:31

Think about that—God wants to save you from those who question your motives, your sincerity, even your worth as a person. And He stands by your side to defend you! God is, of course, above everything. But in Jesus Christ, He became like us and understands the temptations, fears, and weaknesses we face. Then He sent His Holy Spirit to live in our hearts. God couldn't get any closer to us than that.

2 CHRONICLES 9:29–12:16; ACTS 21:33–22:16;
PSALM 110:1–3

And now why tarriest thou? arise, and be baptized,
and wash away thy sins, calling on the name of the Lord.
ACTS 22:16

"Wash away thy sins. . . ." Sounds too easy and too good to be true, doesn't it? Yet God promises He'll erase all our misdeeds if only we call on Him. God doesn't ask us to become perfect, sinless beings to be saved. He doesn't require any heroic acts or amazing feats. All we need to do is believe His promise. It doesn't get any simpler than that!

Bible reading:

2 Chronicles 13–15; Acts 22:17–23:11;
Psalm 110:4–7

*The Lord is with you, while ye be with him;
and if ye seek him, he will be found of you.*
2 Chronicles 15:2

Words that represent immovable objects often
are used to describe God: Rock, Cornerstone,
Foundation. He was, and is, and always will be.
This is important to remember when it feels like
our heavenly Father is far away. The fact is, He
hasn't moved. We have. Get back into prayer and
into His will—look for Him and He won't hide
from you.

*And they came to the chief priests and elders,
and said, We have bound ourselves under a great curse,
that we will eat nothing until we have slain Paul.*

ACTS 23:14

What ever happened to the forty-plus Jews who promised to fast until they had killed the apostle Paul? Since their plot failed, they may have been a very hungry bunch. Did any of them take their promise so seriously that they starved to death? When we make promises—to God, to ourselves, to our family and friends—how seriously do we take them?

Bible reading:

2 Chronicles 18–19; Acts 24:22–25:12;
Psalm 112

*Take heed what ye do: for ye judge not for man,
but for the LORD, who is with you in the judgment.*

2 Chronicles 19:6

❖━━━❖━━━❖

From time to time, we have to make some pretty
heavy decisions based on right and wrong. Whether
it's at the office, at home, or at church, it isn't
always easy to make the right decisions—especially
when people try to influence our way of thinking.
God promises to be there with us as we make those
hard choices. He will give us the guidance we need
to make them wise ones (Proverbs 4:7).

Bible reading:

2 Chronicles 20–21; Acts 25:13–27; Psalm 113

O Lord God of our fathers, art not thou God in heaven?
and rulest not thou over all the kingdoms of the heathen?
and in thine hand is there not power and might,
so that none is able to withstand thee?

2 Chronicles 20:6

———※———※———※———

Isn't it interesting how often we, as Christians, lose sight of the fact that we already know we're on the winning side? The fact is, nothing and no one—not even Satan himself—is strong enough to stand against Yahweh. His power and strength are matchless, and His love and concern for His children is limitless.

Bible reading:

2 CHRONICLES 22–23; ACTS 26; PSALM 114

*Delivering thee from the people, and from the
Gentiles, unto whom now I send thee.*

ACTS 26:17

⋯⋯⋯◆⋯⋯⋯

As long as God has a job for you, you're
indestructible. Jesus promised Paul that the great
apostle would be safe from both Jews and non-Jews
(in other words, *everyone*) while he traveled around
preaching the Gospel. When Paul's job was done,
he looked forward to being with Jesus in heaven,
which is "far better" (Philippians 1:23). There's
never a reason for worry—in Christ, you can't lose!

Bible reading:

2 Chronicles 24:1–25:16; Acts 27:1–20;
Psalm 115:1–10

*Not unto us, O Lord, not unto us, but unto thy name
give glory, for thy mercy, and for thy truth's sake.*
Psalm 115:1

The Bible is filled with tributes to God's holy name. His name is holy and reverent (Psalm 111:9), an everlasting name (Isaiah 63:12), and a name above all other names (Philippians 2:9–10). Yet on any given day, we hear God's name used in ways that are less than worshipful. Today, let's praise—really praise—His wonderful name and thank Him for all His glorious promises.

Bible reading:

2 Chronicles 25:17–27:9; Acts 27:21–28:6;
Psalm 115:11–18

He will bless them that fear the Lord,
both small and great.

Psalm 115:13

Powerhouse CEO. Dedicated office manager. Elementary schoolteacher. Stay-at-home mom. Whatever your profession—and no matter how the world may view it—the Lord considers you an equal to everyone else when it comes to serving Him. He'll reward you in the same manner as all others who revere Him. Nowhere else can you get fair treatment like that!

*I love the Lord, because he hath heard my voice and my
supplications. Because he hath inclined his ear unto
me, therefore will I call upon him as long as I live.*

Psalm 116:1–2

"He hath inclined his ear unto me." No matter how
trivial, the Lord promises to listen to your prayers.
He wants you to draw near to Him—to talk with Him
about everything on your heart (James 4:8). He won't
put you on hold. He won't ask you to come back at
a later time. He won't tune you out. It's a promise
you can count on!

Bible reading:

*To all that be in Rome,
beloved of God, called to be saints.*

Romans 1:7

Have you ever had a special article of clothing or favorite type of food that is reserved for special occasions? We like to set apart certain parts of our lives to keep them fresh, special, different. God does the same thing with His children. When we accept His gift of grace, we are set apart and hold a special place in the Father's heart.

Bible reading:

2 CHRONICLES 31–32; ROMANS 1:18–32; PSALM 117

The truth of the LORD endureth for ever.

PSALM 117:2

All good things, it is said, must come to an end. But that's really not true. This Bible promise assures us that God's Word will last forever. In a world of rapid change and disposable everything, it's comforting to know that our faith is built on the firm, never-changing foundation of "the truth of the Lord." It is permanently recorded in heaven, never to change (Psalm 119:89).

Bible reading:

2 Chronicles 33:1–34:7; Romans 2;
Psalm 118:1–18

There is no respect of persons with God.

Romans 2:11

Rich or poor. Confident or unsure. Man or woman. Joyful or unhappy. Beautiful or plain. The world will judge your worth based on those things and more. But God loves you. . .and He loves you just as much as the next person. Nothing you can say or do could make Him love you any less. His arms are open to you now. Call out to Him and bask in the warmth and comfort of His unconditional love.

Bible reading:

2 Chronicles 34:8–35:19; Romans 3:1–26;
Psalm 118:19–23

Let God be true, but every man a liar; as it is written,
That thou mightest be justified in thy sayings,
and mightest overcome when thou art judged.

Romans 3:4

When one person causes another pain or disappointment, it's easy to question the goodness of God. Why would He let someone cause such heartache? In a world so full of deceit, how can God be truly pure and blameless? The truth is that God's morality doesn't depend on human morality. As lying and evil festers on earth, God does not, and will not, ever change.

Bible reading:

2 Chronicles 35:20–36:23; Romans 3:27–4:25;
Psalm 118:24–29

Thou art my God, and I will praise thee:
thou art my God, I will exalt thee.

Psalm 118:28

✦ ━━━━━ ✦

The psalm writer promised to thank God—an activity that definitely belongs in our lives today. The apostle Paul couldn't be much clearer about that: "In every thing give thanks: for this is the will of God in Christ Jesus concerning you" (1 Thessalonians 5:18). Now that you know the expectation, will you follow through?

Bible reading:

Ezra 1–3; Romans 5; Psalm 119:1–8

That as sin hath reigned unto death, even so might grace reign through righteousness unto eternal life by Jesus Christ our Lord.

Romans 5:21

God's power and love covers all sin—from those little white lies to our deepest, darkest, most shameful sins. We don't ever have to fear the punishment of sin, which is death, because He sent His Son to die for us so that we could have eternal life in heaven with Him (John 3:16). Believe in Him. Accept His forgiveness. And look forward to your eternal home.

Knowing this, that our old man is crucified with him, that the body of sin might be destroyed, that henceforth we should not serve sin.

ROMANS 6:6

Imagine working for a boss named Sin. Along with being demanding and enslaving, Sin keeps its employees chained to an existence that ultimately leads to death. God promises freedom from Sin's dead-end job—freedom through Christ's blood that sets God's "employees," His children, on the fast track of success: eternal life in heaven.

Bible reading:

 EZRA 6:1–7:26; ROMANS 7:7–25; PSALM 119:17–32

I thank God through Jesus Christ our Lord.
So then with the mind I myself serve the law of God.

ROMANS 7:25

Do bad thoughts, attitudes, or habits get you down? You're in good company. Even the apostle Paul—missionary, miracle worker, Bible author—struggled to do the right things. But Paul ended his true confession with this exciting promise: "With the mind I myself serve the law of God." Never doubt that God, "which hath begun a good work in you will perform it until the day of Jesus Christ" (Philippians 1:6).

Bible reading:

EZRA 7:27–9:4; ROMANS 8:1–27; PSALM 119:33–40

Teach me, O LORD, the way of thy statutes;
and I shall keep it unto the end.

PSALM 119:33

There's an implied "if" in this promise: "O Lord, *if* you teach me Your Law, I'll obey it." Is the psalm writer being presumptuous? Not really. God is ready and willing to teach us His truth—and, as we learn more and more of His ways, we should be more and more inclined to obey them. As verse 11 of Psalm 119 says, "Thy word have I hid in mine heart, that I might not sin against thee."

Bible reading:

Ezra 9:5–10:44; Romans 8:28–39;
Psalm 119:41–64

*For I am persuaded, that neither death, nor life,
nor angels, nor principalities, nor powers, nor things
present, nor things to come, nor height, nor depth,
nor any other creature, shall be able to separate us from
the love of God, which is in Christ Jesus our Lord.*

Romans 8:38–39

When things go wrong in life, we may feel as though we've been abandoned by God. But we can find strength and comfort in today's scripture, for God has promised that His love is more powerful than anything in the world—stronger even than death! Our Lord will never keep His love from us, no matter what circumstances life may bring our way. There's no other love like that.

Bible reading:

NEHEMIAH 1:1–3:16; ROMANS 9:1–18;
PSALM 119:65–72

The law of thy mouth is better unto me
than thousands of gold and silver.
PSALM 119:72

Nearly every American owns or has access to a copy of the Holy Bible—many even have two or three copies of varying versions. Because of this, twenty-first-century Christians must be careful to not take the Bible for granted. God's words, instruction, wisdom, and encouragement are worth far more than the retail price assigned to the bar code on the cover.

Bible reading:

Nehemiah 3:17–5:13; Romans 9:19–33;
Psalm 119:73–80

I know, O Lord, that thy judgments are right,
and that thou in faithfulness hast afflicted me.
Psalm 119:75

We don't like the idea of punishment. But God knows it helps us grow to maturity—so He's faithful to provide the discipline we need. "We have had fathers of our flesh which corrected us, and we gave them reverence," the book of Hebrews says. "Shall we not much rather be in subjection unto the Father of spirits, and live?" (12:9). The hard things of life may well be God's promised discipline for our good.

Bible reading:

NEHEMIAH 5:14–7:73; ROMANS 10:1–13;
PSALM 119:81–88

*For whosoever shall call upon the name
of the Lord shall be saved.*

ROMANS 10:13

The punishment for sin is death. And we're all sinners (Romans 3:23), so does that leave us without hope? God's Word says that all we need to do is believe, and we'll be saved from death. He loves us so much that He sent His only Son to redeem us (1 John 4:9; John 3:16). He has cleared us from all blame and debt—He has freed us from the bonds of sin. He has provided us with the only true source of hope in this world—His Son. Thank Him today for this amazing gift.

Bible reading:

*So then faith cometh by hearing,
and hearing by the word of God.*

ROMANS 10:17

Preaching of the good news doesn't always come from behind a pulpit. Faith can be born out of the influence of a friend witnessing to another, a Sunday school teacher, a youth sponsor, a mentor, a coach. God promises to plant those seeds of faith in receptive hearts. Our job is to seek out preaching opportunities.

Bible reading:

NEHEMIAH 9:6–10:27; ROMANS 11:25–12:8;
PSALM 119:105–120

*[Thou] hast performed thy words;
for thou art righteous.*
NEHEMIAH 9:8

Many times throughout the Bible, we see reminders of God's faithfulness. When He promises, He delivers. In this passage, the Jewish leader Nehemiah is reminding the people of God's promises and how He lived up to His word. That's a good exercise for us today—regularly reviewing God's faithfulness in our lives will give us hope and confidence for whatever circumstances we may face.

Bible reading:

NEHEMIAH 10:28–12:26; ROMANS 12:9–13:7;
PSALM 119:121–128

Let every soul be subject unto the higher powers.
For there is no power but of God: the powers
that be are ordained of God.

ROMANS 13:1

While we vote our government leaders into
office, God's Word says that "the powers that be
are ordained of God." So while we may fret and
question why some officials are in office, we must
turn our concerns over to God. He has plans
that we may not understand. . .but we may find
comfort in the knowledge that the power held by
the leaders of our country has been given by Him.
Say a prayer for our leaders today.

Bible reading:

Nehemiah 12:27–13:31; Romans 13:8–14:12;
Psalm 119:129–136

Love worketh no ill to his neighbour:
therefore love is the fulfilling of the law.
Romans 13:10

The Bible tells us that love covers many sins
(1 Peter 4:8). Here, Paul takes that idea a step
further by saying that if we start out by loving
others, we won't fall into sins of killing, stealing,
lying, and coveting. True Christian love means
sincerely caring for others. Such love leaves no
room for sins that could hurt another person.

Bible reading:

ESTHER 1:1–2:18; ROMANS 14:13–15:13;
PSALM 119:137–152

For he that in these things serveth Christ is
acceptable to God, and approved of men.
ROMANS 14:18

God is pleased with us when we show love to others.
When we put the needs and interests of others
first, when we go out of our way to help the weak,
when we seek peace among our fellow Christians—
God has promised that He'll be happy with us.
And when God is happy with us, how could we
be unhappy?

Bible reading:

ESTHER 2:19–5:14; ROMANS 15:14–21;
PSALM 119:153–168

*Thy word is true from the beginning: and every one of
thy righteous judgments endureth for ever.*
PSALM 119:160

Nothing lasts forever. . .except God's Word. Jesus
Himself said, "Heaven and earth shall pass away,
but my words shall not pass away" (Matthew 24:35).
That's because every word of the Bible was penned
by men who were inspired by God (2 Timothy
3:16). When you think about this, daily devotions
take on a whole new meaning. Yes, God's promises
last forever!

Bible reading:

ESTHER 6–8; ROMANS 15:22–33;
PSALM 119:169–176

*My tongue shall speak of thy word: for all thy
commandments are righteousness.*
PSALM 119:172

Our world is a topsy-turvy roller-coaster ride when it comes to right and wrong, good and bad. Our coworkers, our friends, and our children are bombarded with mixed messages about morality. We can hold fast to the truth of God's Word when we need guidance for life. He'll steer us in the right direction. And we can have an impact on the world by "singing" praises about the blessings He's poured out on us.

Bible reading:

ESTHER 9–10; ROMANS 16; PSALM 120–122

*And the God of peace shall bruise Satan
under your feet shortly.*

ROMANS 16:20

Satan's day is coming. It's just a matter of time.
While God's children live in a fallen world and deal
with the temptations that Satan orchestrates every
day, it's sometimes hard not to feel discouraged.
Although the final God versus Satan showdown
is still to come, God promises His children small
day-to-day victories over Satan—with His help.

Who shall also confirm you unto the end, that ye may
be blameless in the day of our Lord Jesus Christ.
1 CORINTHIANS 1:8

One of the most encouraging promises of the
Bible is this: God Himself gives us the strength
to live the Christian life. Sure, we're responsible
for making the right choices and doing the right
thing, but it's God who gives us both the desire
and the power to do so. When God started a good
work in your life, He intended to see it through
(see Philippians 1:6).

Bible reading:

JOB 4–6; 1 CORINTHIANS 1:26–2:16;
PSALM 124–125

*But God hath chosen the foolish things of the world to
confound the wise; and God hath chosen the weak things
of the world to confound the things which are mighty;
And base things of the world, and things which are
despised, hath God chosen, yea, and things which
are not, to bring to nought things that are.*

1 CORINTHIANS 1:27–28

The world often labels Christians as weak and
fanatical rather than powerful and down to earth.
But because the Lord stands opposed to the world
and everything it upholds (1 John 2:15–16), we
can remain confident that God is behind us as
we hold fast to our faith and to the promise that
He will strengthen us and protect us from Satan
(2 Thessalonians 3:3).

Bible reading:

Job 7–9; 1 Corinthians 3; Psalm 126–127

Know ye not that ye are the temple of God,
and that the Spirit of God dwelleth in you? . . .
For the temple of God is holy, which temple ye are.
1 Corinthians 3:16–17

Holiness isn't something to be earned or achieved. A Christian can never be good enough, pure enough, or devout enough to somehow earn holiness. God's Spirit lives inside believers. God also says that His house is holy, so we as Christians, through none of our own doing, are holy.

Bible reading:

Job 10–13; 1 Corinthians 4:1–13; Psalm 128–129

Blessed is every one that feareth the LORD;
that walketh in his ways.

Psalm 128:1

❖

Everyone wants to be happy, and here is God's prescription for joy: honor Him with fear, and walk in His ways. When we do what God tells us to do, happiness follows. Not necessarily wealth, or pleasure, or ease, but the deep-seated contentment that the apostle Paul described in Philippians 4:11. That's a promise worth noting!

Bible reading:

Job 14–16; 1 Corinthians 4:14–5:13; Psalm 130

But there is forgiveness with thee,
that thou mayest be feared.

Psalm 130:4

Forgiving others is a challenge, isn't it? Sometimes
the hurt runs so deep, we just can't seem to let go. But
we can find a great example to follow when it comes
to forgiving others: the Lord forgets our mistakes as
quickly as we can ask His forgiveness (Isaiah 43:25).
He even promises to remove our sins "as far as the
east is from the west" (Psalm 103:12). Ask the Lord
to touch your heart and allow the spirit of forgiveness
to envelop your soul today.

Bible reading:

Job 17–20; 1 Corinthians 6; Psalm 131

What? know ye not that your body is the temple of the
Holy Ghost which is in you, which ye have of God,
and ye are not your own? For ye are bought with
a price: therefore glorify God in your body,
and in your spirit, which are God's.

1 Corinthians 6:19–20

❖

God laid down the entire payment—the life of His only Son—to pay for the freedom of every man, woman, boy, and girl who ever has, and ever will, live on earth. In any normal transaction, this purchase would be complete. But God knew the relationship He desires with humans wouldn't be real love unless we willingly accept the gift He offers. Only when we surrender ourselves to God is the transaction complete.

Bible reading:

JOB 21–23; 1 CORINTHIANS 7:1–16; PSALM 132

For I would that all men were even as I myself.
But every man hath his proper gift of God,
one after this manner, and another after that.

1 CORINTHIANS 7:7

In this passage, the apostle Paul praises singleness. People who aren't married, he says, can devote more of their time and energy to God's service. But Paul also realized that many—likely *most*—people would prefer to wed. And he acknowledged that people have different "gifts." God has promised to "gift" every believer with certain abilities and skills, then to judge them only according to their own—and nobody else's—gifts (1 Corinthians 12).

Bible reading:

*He bindeth up the waters in his thick clouds; and the
cloud is not rent under them. He holdeth back the face
of his throne, and spreadeth his cloud upon it.
He hath compassed the waters with bounds,
until the day and night come to an end.*

JOB 26:8–10

When Job uttered these words, he had lost his
entire family, all his property, and his health. But
instead of raising his fist to heaven in anger, Job
praised God! Like Job, when things get rough, we
can look to God's creation to see evidence of His
presence. We can remember God's promise to
Noah that those things we take for granted will
always be (Genesis 8:22).

Bible reading:

Job 28–30; 1 Corinthians 8; Psalm 135

But to us there is but one God, the Father, of whom are all things, and we in him; and one Lord Jesus Christ, by whom are all things, and we by him.

1 Corinthians 8:6

Think about all the things you love—your family, your job, chocolate-chip-cookie-dough ice cream, sunrises—and remember where all these things came from. God, our Father, gives us "all things." These "things" are blessings from Him. So the next time you bite into that delicious ice-cream cone, give thanks. He'd love to hear from you.

Bible reading:

*To him that made great lights: for his mercy endureth
for ever: the sun to rule by day: for his mercy endureth
for ever: the moon and stars to rule by night:
for his mercy endureth for ever.*

Psalm 136:7–9

Try to list all your blessings, and you'll probably
soon realize you can't keep a running tally. There
are too many to number! God created all things with
only the best for us in mind. Like the moon and
the stars, our "nightlights" in the darkness, which
He made especially for us to enjoy. Everything He
created stems from his loving-kindness, which has
no end.

Bible reading:

JOB 34–36; 1 CORINTHIANS 9:19–10:13;
PSALM 136:10–26

---

*There hath no temptation taken you but such as is
common to man: but God is faithful, who will not suffer
you to be tempted above that ye are able; but will
with the temptation also make a way to escape,
that ye may be able to bear it.*

1 CORINTHIANS 10:13

✦

Just like the tantalizing scent of warm chocolate-chip cookies baking, sin's temptations tickle our senses and desires every day, sometimes several times a day. Paul reminds us that when it feels like there's no way to avoid sin, God is faithful to keep temptations at a level we can deal with. What's more, He promises a way out of the situation—we just have to keep our eyes open to His will.

Bible reading:

Ye cannot drink the cup of the Lord, and the cup of devils: ye cannot be partakers of the Lord's table, and of the table of devils.

1 Corinthians 10:21

Never try to convince yourself that "a little sin" is acceptable. While the apostle Paul was making a theological argument about food sacrificed to idols, this "promise" sounds much like Jesus' warning that "no man can serve two masters: for either he will hate the one, and love the other; or else he will hold to the one, and despise the other" (Matthew 6:24). Don't have a divided mind. Live for God—and God alone.

Bible reading:

JOB 40–42; 1 CORINTHIANS 11:2–34; PSALM 138

I know that thou canst do every thing,
and that no thought can be withholden from thee.
JOB 42:2

❖

Whatever God's plan, no one and nothing can stop Him. He can do absolutely anything—even the seemingly impossible. His wisdom and power rise above everything in this world. Remember this promise for your own life, because God has a plan just for you—a plan for your future—and nothing can get in the way of it (Jeremiah 29:11).

Bible reading:

For our comely parts have no need: but God hath tempered the body together, having given more abundant honour to that part which lacked. That there should be no schism in the body; but that the members should have the same care one for another. And whether one member suffer, all the members suffer with it; or one member be honoured, all the members rejoice with it.

1 Corinthians 12:24–26

God yearns for unity in His church. One way unity happens is when a church member is dependent on another. This is why He grants His children their own unique gifts, and why He promises care to the people who need it most. When we work inside God's will, the church is the living embodiment of God's kingdom on earth.

ECCLESIASTES 3:16–6:12;
1 CORINTHIANS 12:27–13:13; PSALM 139:7–18

All go unto one place; all are of the dust,
and all turn to dust again.

ECCLESIASTES 3:20

On its face, this "promise" seems a bit dreary: we're all going to die. But a little perspective can turn the negative into a positive. We're returning to dust because that's what we're made of—by God Himself (Genesis 2:7). He knows we're only dust (Psalm 103:14), yet he's able to form us into things of real worth, just like a potter molding clay (Isaiah 64:8).

Bible reading:

*In the day of prosperity be joyful, but in the day
of adversity consider: God also hath set
the one over against the other.*

ECCLESIASTES 7:14

It's easy to think that when all is well, God is on our side. He's blessing us. He's seeing to all our needs, and we're happy. But when trouble comes, we often feel as though God has left us alone to fend for ourselves. What's harder to see is that God sometimes allows us to go through the rough spots only to bring us to a better place in our lives, and in our relationship with Him. In the tough times, He hasn't abandoned us; He's helping us to grow.

Bible reading:

ECCLESIASTES 9:13–12:14;
1 CORINTHIANS 14:23–15:11; PSALM 140:1–8

Fear God, and keep his commandments: for this is the whole duty of man. For God shall bring every work into judgment, with every secret thing, whether it be good, or whether it be evil.

ECCLESIASTES 12:13–14

Judges who preside over earthly courts aren't perfect. Only God can be the perfect Judge, who knows all, sees all, and exists everywhere. His judgment promise spans more than just condemning the guilty—He will evaluate every act, even the good, and reward or punish accordingly.

Bible reading:

SONG OF SOLOMON 1–4; 1 CORINTHIANS 15:12–34;
PSALM 140:9–13

*For as in Adam all die, even so in Christ
shall all be made alive.*

1 CORINTHIANS 15:22

❖

If you've accepted Jesus as your Savior, this verse
promises you an exciting future. You're in line for
an "everlasting life" (John 3:16), and there won't be
any "death, neither sorrow, nor crying, neither shall
there be any more pain" (Revelation 21:4). You'll
live with God Himself (Revelation 21:3), enjoying
eternity as His beloved child (Revelation 21:7). Wow
. . .do you have goose bumps?

Bible reading:

*But thanks be to God, which giveth us
the victory through our Lord Jesus Christ.*

1 CORINTHIANS 15:57

❖━━━◆━━━❖

When John the Baptist saw Jesus approaching, he remarked, "Behold the Lamb of God, which taketh away the sin of the world" (John 1:29). A few years later, Jesus literally overcame sin and death when He hung on the cross for the sins of humanity. Take hold of the power of Jesus today; ask Him to guide your steps.

Bible reading:

ISAIAH 1–2; 1 CORINTHIANS 16; PSALM 142

Come now, and let us reason together, saith the LORD:
though your sins be as scarlet, they shall be as white
as snow; though they be red like crimson,
they shall be as wool.

ISAIAH 1:18

You know how hard it is to remove a stubborn stain. You spot-treat it. You scrub it. You retreat and rewash it, only to give up in the end. Our sins are like those hard-to-remove stains. But even though God says our sins are bright red, they can be made "as white as snow. . .as wool." He promises to wash our sin stains—to remove them permanently the first time around. No rewashing needed!

Bible reading:

ISAIAH 3–5; 2 CORINTHIANS 1:1–11; PSALM 143:1–6

And whether we be afflicted, it is for your consolation and salvation, which is effectual in the enduring of the same sufferings which we also suffer: or whether we be comforted, it is for your consolation and salvation.

2 CORINTHIANS 1:6

It's no secret that Paul went through his share of trouble during his ministry. From imprisonment and persecution to a shipwreck and a mysterious physical handicap (2 Corinthians 12:7), this great missionary of the Christian faith endured years of difficulty to spread the Gospel. But throughout his darkest of days, God provided strength—the same strength offered to Christians to endure troubles in order to share the love of Christ.

Bible reading:

Isaiah 6–8; 2 Corinthians 1:12–2:4;
Psalm 143:7–12

---

*For all the promises of God in [Jesus] are yea,
and in him Amen, unto the glory of God by us.*
2 Corinthians 1:20

Prophecies in essence are promises, and God said throughout the Old Testament that He would send a Savior for all people. In familiar passages like Genesis 3, Isaiah 9, and Micah 5, God hinted or clearly stated that He would provide a way of salvation for sinful humanity. And in Jesus Christ, all those promises were fulfilled!

To whom ye forgive any thing, I forgive also: for if I forgave any thing, to whom I forgave it, for your sakes forgave I it in the person of Christ.

2 Corinthians 2:10

Past hurts have their way of getting stuck in "repeat mode" in our minds, which makes it more difficult to forgive the people who have hurt us. While forgiving others isn't always easy, God calls us to forgive just as He forgives us (Colossians 3:13). He loves us enough to overlook our shortcomings; all He asks is that we do the same for others (Mark 11:25). Praise God today for His amazing love, and ask Him to help you pass that love on.

Bible reading:

Isaiah 11–13; 2 Corinthians 3; Psalm 145

*And the spirit of the LORD shall rest upon him,
the spirit of wisdom and understanding, the spirit
of counsel and might, the spirit of knowledge
and of the fear of the LORD.*

Isaiah 11:2

❖

As Jesus developed from a boy into a man, He grew strong in mind and body and in favor with God and men (Luke 2:52). Generations before He made His earthly appearance, God knew exactly how Jesus would be on earth. Is it any surprise that God has known us—our personalities, our strengths, our character flaws—since the beginning of time?

For I will rise up against them, saith the LORD of hosts,
and cut off from Babylon the name, and remnant,
and son, and nephew, saith the LORD.

Isaiah 14:22

Babylon was once one of the greatest cities of the world—until God made good on this promise against it. The fulfillment of Isaiah's prophecy against Babylon proved God's absolute power over the kings and peoples of earth, just as He says in Psalm 22:28: "For the kingdom is the LORD's: and he is the governor among the nations." Whatever you read in the news today, remember this: God is in control.

Bible reading:

Isaiah 17–19; 2 Corinthians 5; Psalm 147:1–11

For we know that if our earthly house of this tabernacle
were dissolved, we have a building of God, an house
not made with hands, eternal in the heavens.

2 Corinthians 5:1

Just like old houses that need repair, our bodies wear out over time. Our joints ache. Our bodies are destroyed by injury and illness. And although our earthly bodies will eventually shut down completely, we can rejoice in the promise of a new body—a heavenly body created just for us. . . one that will last for eternity. The aches and pains of this world are only temporary. That's God's promise to us!

DAY 261

Bible reading:

Isaiah 20–23; 2 Corinthians 6; Psalm 147:12–20

Wherefore come out from among them, and be ye separate, saith the Lord, and touch not the unclean thing; and I will receive you. And will be a Father unto you, and ye shall be my sons and daughters, saith the Lord Almighty.

2 Corinthians 6:17–18

God asks His children to flee from sin not because He's a killjoy or a stick-in-the-mud. The truth is, God wants to receive every person into His embrace, but because of His goodness and His perfection, He cannot embrace someone who harbors sin in his or her heart. Purity—with the help of Christ's cleansing blood—earns God's fatherhood.

Bible reading:

Isaiah 24:1–26:19; 2 Corinthians 7; Psalm 148

He hath also stablished them for ever and ever:
he hath made a decree which shall not pass.

Psalm 148:6

You can count on God's Word. The eternal God has spoken an eternal Law—and we can know the "rules of the game." There will be no surprises, in this life or the next, because God's Word won't change or disappear. In a world that changes so quickly, it's nice to know we have something solid to grasp—the very Word of God Himself.

Bible reading:

ISAIAH 26:20–28:29; 2 CORINTHIANS 8;
PSALM 149–150

*Therefore thus saith the Lord GOD, Behold,
I lay in Zion for a foundation a stone, a tried stone,
a precious corner stone, a sure foundation:
he that believeth shall not make haste.*

ISAIAH 28:16

The prophet Isaiah was writing about Jesus Christ, hundreds of years before His arrival on earth. Jesus used the same imagery when He called Himself "the stone which the builders rejected" (Luke 20:17). Jesus is not only the Foundation of His church—He can be the Cornerstone of our lives, if we let Him. Don't be afraid of building your life on Him.

Bible reading:

And God is able to make all grace abound toward you;
that ye, always having all sufficiency in all things,
may abound to every good work.

2 Corinthians 9:8

❖

Do you always feel like you never have quite enough? After barely covering bills and basic necessities, how could God expect you to give anything away? Yet, if you turn control of your needs over to God, He promises to meet your needs—and then some. Step out in faith, and prepare to be amazed at the abundance He has in store for you.

Bible reading:

But he that glorieth, let him glory in the Lord.
For not he that commendeth himself is approved,
but whom the Lord commendeth.

2 Corinthians 10:17–18

To the world, self-confidence and self-assurance are vital characteristics to possess. Self-esteem separates the successful from the unsuccessful and the beautiful from the ugly. But God sees a person's worth in a different light. *"Find your self-worth in what I have done to change you,"* God says. *"The grace extended through the blood shed by My Son is what guarantees your importance in My kingdom."*

Bible reading:

Isaiah 34–36; 2 Corinthians 11;
Proverbs 1:23–26

*Therefore it is no great thing if [Satan's] ministers
also be transformed as the ministers of righteousness;
whose end shall be according to their works.*

2 Corinthians 11:15

❖ ─── ❖ ─── ❖

Are you angered when people use the name of Jesus
to lead others astray? Those the apostle Paul calls
"false apostles" have done much harm, since the
very beginning of the Christian church. But selfish
and wicked people—serving the devil himself—will
not ultimately win. God has promised to right all
wrongs in the end (Matthew 25:41).

Bible reading:

Isaiah 37–38; 2 Corinthians 12:1–10;
Proverbs 1:27–33

*And he said unto me, My grace is sufficient for thee:
for my strength is made perfect in weakness.*

2 Corinthians 12:9

Life would be better if only I had. . . More money.
A bigger house. A nicer car. A new career. Sound
familiar? But God promises us that our lives can
be joyful and complete without all these earthly
things (Matthew 6:19–21)—if we only draw near
to Him. He is *really* all we'll ever need.

Bible reading:

Isaiah 39–40; 2 Corinthians 12:11–13:14;
Proverbs 2:1–15

*He giveth power to the faint; and to them
that have no might he increaseth strength.*

Isaiah 40:29

Every elementary school playground has its token
bully—the kid who likes to pick on children smaller
than him just because he can. God offers strength
and power to the kids getting bullied—and the poor
and weak of the world—to withstand the bullying
of Satan. He won't leave the weak unarmed.

Bible reading:

ISAIAH 41–42; GALATIANS 1; PROVERBS 2:16–22

Behold my servant, whom I uphold;
mine elect, in whom my soul delighteth;
I have put my spirit upon him.

ISAIAH 42:1

Hundreds of years after this prophecy was written, it was fulfilled at the baptism of Jesus. At the Jordan River, the Holy Spirit descended on Jesus like a dove—and a voice from heaven boomed, "This is my beloved Son, in whom I am well pleased" (Matthew 3:17). Amazingly, we can experience much the same thing: in salvation, we too receive God's Spirit (Acts 2:38). And we become His much-loved children (Galatians 3:26).

Bible reading:

Fear not: for I have redeemed thee,
I have called thee by thy name; thou art mine.

Isaiah 43:1

In this life, people will desert and disappoint us. But there is One who promises never to abandon us in our time of need. Our Creator, who calls us by name and claims us as His own, will shelter and strengthen us. He'll walk closely by our side, if we only ask Him to. Call out to Him now; He's waiting to hear from you.

Bible reading:

Isaiah 44:21–46:13; Galatians 3:1–18;
Proverbs 3:13–26

*Happy is the man that findeth wisdom, and the man
that getteth understanding. For the merchandise of
it is better than the merchandise of silver,
and the gain thereof than fine gold.*

Proverbs 3:13–14

Proverbs says the Lord built the earth by wisdom and
the heavens by understanding (Proverbs 3:19). As
Christians, we're called to strive for such wisdom—
heavenly wisdom. God promises that getting His
understanding is better than silver and gold.

Bible reading:

The wise shall inherit glory:
but shame shall be the promotion of fools.

PROVERBS 3:35

Notice the word *shall* in this promise. It means something is *going* to happen, though it doesn't say when. In our backward world, fools are often honored while the wise are sometimes shamed. But God will ultimately correct that injustice. In the meantime, be wise (see James 3:17).

Bible reading:

Isaiah 49:14–51:23; Galatians 4:1–11;
Proverbs 4:1–19

*And because ye are sons, God hath sent forth the Spirit
of his Son into your hearts, crying, Abba, Father.*

Galatians 4:6

Sometimes when young children clamor for a parent's attention, they're really just making sure that their mother or father is there. When we have the Holy Spirit inside us, the desire to connect with our heavenly Father becomes as intense as that of a child with its earthly parents. God longs to hear from you. . .and He longs to show He cares (1 Peter 5:7).

Bible reading:

Isaiah 52–54; Galatians 4:12–31;
Proverbs 4:20–27

Keep thy heart with all diligence;
for out of it are the issues of life.

Proverbs 4:23

What's important in your life? Your career? Your car? Your house? Your family and friends? God promises that the most important things life has to offer will be yours if you keep your heart pure and focused on Him. Ask Him to help you keep your focus today, and anticipate the good things He will shower upon you.

Bible reading:

Isaiah 55–57; Galatians 5; Proverbs 5:1–14

So shall my word be that goeth forth out of my mouth:
it shall not return unto me void, but it shall accomplish
that which I please, and it shall prosper
in the thing whereto I sent it.

Isaiah 55:11

God's Word is described in Hebrews 4:12 as being sharper than a sword that cuts both ways. John 1:1 also tells us that the Word (Christ) existed from the very beginning. The Word was with God. The Father made good on His promise. Jesus left heaven to come to earth to endure shame, ridicule, and death. He carried out God's plan for salvation.

Bible reading:

Isaiah 58–59; Galatians 6; Proverbs 5:15–23

Behold, the LORD's hand is not shortened, that it cannot save; neither his ear heavy, that it cannot hear.

Isaiah 59:1

God is always capable of helping us. His hand is powerful and can save. His ears are open to our cries. But sin in our lives can create barriers between us and God (Isaiah 59:2). Even a man's lack of respect toward his wife will cause prayers to be "hindered" (1 Peter 3:7). God has promised that He can help. Let's not negate that offer by our own sin.

Bible reading:

According as he hath chosen us in him before the foundation of the world, that we should be holy and without blame before him in love.

Ephesians 1:4

❖

Do you think you're pretty special? Well, you are! You are so special that you were handpicked by God—even before He created the world. Pretty amazing stuff, huh? His love for us is so great that nothing in this world can separate us from Him—not now, not ever. Thank God for this one-of-a-kind love that you can't find anywhere but through Him.

Bible reading:

ISAIAH 63:1–65:16; EPHESIANS 2; PROVERBS 6:6–19

For by grace are ye saved through faith;
and that not of yourselves: it is the gift of God.

EPHESIANS 2:8

We're programmed at a young age that in order to
gain something, we have to earn it—that the only
way to accomplish anything is by blood, sweat,
tears, and hard work. Salvation isn't like that.
God tells us simply that His grace isn't earned by
our good works, deeds, or behavior. Salvation is
a gift to people who put their faith in Him.

Bible reading:

For, behold, I create new heavens and a new earth:
and the former shall not be remembered,
nor come into mind.

ISAIAH 65:17

Life can be good. But it can also be hard. At times, "hard" outweighs "good." But a time is coming when God will put all our pain and sorrow behind us, never to be recalled. Even the earth and heavens we know will be changed for the better—completely new and perfect. Since God basically repeated this promise in Revelation 21, it's definitely worth remembering. . .especially on those hard days.

Bible reading:

*And that ye put on the new man, which after God
is created in righteousness and true holiness.*

EPHESIANS 4:24

Become a "new man," not "sort of a different person." Be "Godlike," not "sort of Godlike." We need to put away the old us as we live for Christ and become new through Him (2 Corinthians 5:17). We can't just change a little; He requires that we change wholly and completely for Him. Only then can we have the amazing life He has promised us.

Bible reading:

JEREMIAH 3:1–4:22; EPHESIANS 5; PROVERBS 7:1–5

*For this cause shall a man leave his father
and mother, and shall be joined unto his wife,
and they two shall be one flesh.*

EPHESIANS 5:31

❖

God's desire for unity among Christians begins at home. When a man and woman become husband and wife, His wedding present is creating one out of two. Think of it as the reverse of what He did in the Garden of Eden—instead of creating two distinct beings (Adam and Eve), He makes them one.

Bible reading:

JEREMIAH 4:23–5:31; EPHESIANS 6;
PROVERBS 7:6–27

Knowing that whatsoever good thing any man doeth,
the same shall he receive of the Lord,
whether he be bond or free.

EPHESIANS 6:8

Overworked and underpaid? Not appreciated by your family or friends? Wondering if it's really worth it to do the right thing? This promise provides the encouragement to keep plugging on. Whether anybody else notices or cares about your good work, God does. And His rewards are always the best, anyway.

Bible reading:

JEREMIAH 6:1–7:26; PHILIPPIANS 1:1–26;
PROVERBS 8:1–11

For to me to live is Christ, and to die is gain.

PHILIPPIANS 1:21

To write these words, the apostle Paul had to embrace the promise of John 3:16: "For God so loved the world, that he gave his only begotten Son, that whosoever believeth in him should not perish, but have everlasting life." This doesn't mean we shouldn't live life to the fullest. Rather, we should not fear death because we are confident of God's precious promise.

Bible reading:

JEREMIAH 7:27–9:16; PHILIPPIANS 1:27–2:18;
PROVERBS 8:12–21

I love them that love me; and those that
seek me early shall find me.

PROVERBS 8:17

God isn't some elusive being who is always just beyond our reach. He loves us enough that He's made Himself available 24-7. There's never a time—day or night—that we can't reach Him. We have the comfort of knowing that we never have to be alone now or in the future—guaranteed!

Bible reading:

He hath made the earth by his power, he hath established the world by his wisdom, and hath stretched out the heavens by his discretion. When he uttereth his voice, there is a multitude of waters in the heavens, and he causeth the vapours to ascend from the ends of the earth; he maketh lightnings with rain, and bringeth forth the wind out of his treasures.

JEREMIAH 10:12–13

The nature of God is almost impossible to describe. As loving and as merciful as He is, the Creator of the universe is just as powerful. He's able to manipulate His creation in whatever way He deems best—from the depths of the oceans to the highest of the heavens. As long as we're on His side, we can take comfort in the knowledge that His wrathful power is reserved to defeat Satan.

Bible reading:

JEREMIAH 11:18–13:27; PHILIPPIANS 3;
PROVERBS 9:1–6

*Who shall change our vile body, that it may be
fashioned like unto his glorious body, according to
the working whereby he is able even to
subdue all things unto himself.*

PHILIPPIANS 3:21

"The perfect body." In our society, these words
indicate an idealized (and unrealistic) Hollywood
image. In the Bible, it means we'll someday be like
the resurrected Jesus. God has promised to change
our earthly bodies to be like Christ's—bodies that
will never die again. We'll live forever with Him,
without all the aches, pains, and weariness we
experience now. Aren't you eager to enjoy that
sleek new model?

Bible reading:

JEREMIAH 14–15; PHILIPPIANS 4; PROVERBS 9:7–18

*I can do all things through Christ
which strengtheneth me.*

PHILIPPIANS 4:13

Rely on God to get you through the tough times
. . .because you certainly can't handle everything
on your own. Without Christ, we're weak and
powerless; with Christ, we're strong and mighty.
Ask God today to infuse you with the courage you
need to overcome the obstacles you're facing in
life.

Bible reading:

JEREMIAH 16–17; COLOSSIANS 1:1–23;
PROVERBS 10:1–5

Blessed is the man that trusteth in the LORD, and whose
hope the LORD is. For he shall be as a tree planted by the
waters, and that spreadeth out her roots by the river,
and shall not see when heat cometh, but her leaf shall
be green; and shall not be careful in the year of drought,
neither shall cease from yielding fruit.

JEREMIAH 17:7–8

God promises to be a source of life to men and
women who trust in Him. God doesn't promise that
His water will keep Christians from difficulties—the
heat of drought will come—but He does promise that
the source of life, hope, and strength will always be
there to sustain His children.

Bible reading:

JEREMIAH 18:1–20:6; COLOSSIANS 1:24–2:15;
PROVERBS 10:6–14

*And ye are complete in [Christ], which is the head
of all principality and power.*
COLOSSIANS 2:10

"Self-fulfillment" is a popular idea, and people pursue it through money, power, and the pleasures of life. But only in Jesus are we truly complete. The One who created the universe and keeps it running (Colossians 1:15–20) will actually live in us (John 15:4). This is a promise of ultimate fulfillment. What more could you possibly hope for?

Bible reading:

JEREMIAH 20:7–22:19; COLOSSIANS 2:16–3:4;
PROVERBS 10:15–26

The labour of the righteous tendeth to life:
the fruit of the wicked to sin.

PROVERBS 10:16

A life without God is a life that will surely end in death (Romans 6:23). However, God promises that if we place our faith and trust in Him—and if we live a life in right relationship with Him—we will receive life. And not just a longer life, but an *eternal* life in heaven, free from all the sadness and problems of the world.

Bible reading:

JEREMIAH 22:20–23:40; COLOSSIANS 3:5–4:1;
PROVERBS 10:27–32

And above all these things put on charity,
which is the bond of perfectness.

COLOSSIANS 3:14

❊❊❊

Throughout history, revolutionaries tried to change their circumstances by manipulation, force, and violence. Jesus' take on revolution isn't violent. It isn't hurtful, and it isn't selfish. It's love. He promises unity in love and—even better—He promises that good will be made perfect.

*Riches profit not in the day of wrath:
but righteousness delivereth from death.*

PROVERBS 11:4

No amount of money can protect you from sin and
its punishment. That's the bad news. The good
news is this promise: "Righteousness delivereth
from death." Even better news is that being right
with God doesn't cost us a thing—it's "the gift
of God" given by Jesus (Romans 6:23). Are you
working or worrying for your salvation today?
Don't—just accept and enjoy it.

Bible reading:

JEREMIAH 26–27; 1 THESSALONIANS 1:1–2:8;
PROVERBS 11:12–21

Knowing, brethren beloved, your election of God.
1 THESSALONIANS 1:4

If you panicked every time teams were chosen in phys ed, knowing for sure that you would be picked last, this promise of God is immensely reassuring. Jesus said, "Ye have not chosen me, but I have chosen you, and ordained you, that ye should go and bring forth fruit" (John 15:16). All Christians have the privilege and responsibility to share the good news. We were chosen to love each other (John 15:17).

Bible reading:

Jeremiah 28–29; 1 Thessalonians 2:9–3:13;
Proverbs 11:22–26

*The liberal soul shall be made fat:
and he that watereth shall be watered also himself.*

Proverbs 11:25

Admit it. You sometimes hesitate to give, because you're skeptical about what you'll get in return. But God's Word promises a huge return on your investment: give a lot and receive a lot; help someone and you'll be helped. Be a cheerful giver (2 Corinthians 9:7) and see what happens. God promises you'll be blessed!

Bible reading:

JEREMIAH 30:1–31:22; 1 THESSALONIANS 4:1–5:11;
PROVERBS 11:27–31

And that ye study to be quiet, and to do your
own business, and to work with your own hands,
as we commanded you; that ye may walk honestly
toward them that are without, and that ye
may have lack of nothing.

1 THESSALONIANS 4:11–12

❖━━━◆━━━❖

God asks His children to be good workers—not
lazy, not prone to procrastination. How does
this apply to our Christian witness? As Christ's
ambassadors, every aspect of our lives—including
the forty-plus hours we spend in our careers
each week—should reflect a spirit of ability and
assurance. When non-Christians see Christians
who are capable coworkers, it may open new
opportunities for witnessing.

Bible reading:

JEREMIAH 31:23–32:35; 1 THESSALONIANS 5:12–28;
PROVERBS 12:1–14

*Behold, the days come, saith the LORD, that I will
make a new covenant with the house of Israel,
and with the house of Judah.*

JEREMIAH 31:31

God made a promise through the prophet
Jeremiah that was fulfilled in Jesus Christ: a "new
covenant" that took the place of the Old Testament
laws and sacrifices. Jesus' death and resurrection
broke the power of the law (Romans 8:2–4) and
offered us a new life of spiritual freedom. Aren't
you glad?

Bible reading:

JEREMIAH 32:36–34:7; 2 THESSALONIANS 1–2;
PROVERBS 12:15–20

*Call unto me, and I will answer thee, and show thee
great and mighty things, which thou knowest not.*

JEREMIAH 33:3

The Lord says if we call out to Him, He "will
answer" us. Not He "might answer." Not He
"won't answer." But He *will*! When you talk to God,
open your heart. You can rest assured that He's
listening and that He will offer up the appropriate
response in His perfect timing. You can count
on it.

Lying lips are abomination to the LORD:
but they that deal truly are his delight.

PROVERBS 12:22

Parents often refer to their children as their
"pride and joy." God loves His children with
even more fervent devotion than earthly parents.
When we choose to speak the truth—no matter
the cost and circumstance—God calls us His joy.
It's a daily struggle and decision to choose the
path of truth, but one that will be rewarded now
and in eternity.

Bible reading:

JEREMIAH 36:11–38:13; 1 TIMOTHY 1:1–17;
PROVERBS 13:1–4

*This is a faithful saying, and worthy of all acceptation,
that Christ Jesus came into the world to
save sinners; of whom I am chief.*
1 TIMOTHY 1:15

The apostle Paul spoke for every Bible writer when he proclaimed the truth of his message. In a second letter to Timothy, Paul said, "All scripture is given by inspiration of God" (2 Timothy 3:16). "For the prophecy came not in old time by the will of man," the apostle Peter added, "but holy men of God spake as they were moved by the Holy Ghost" (2 Peter 1:21). You can trust *all* the Bible's promises—because every one comes from God Himself.

Bible reading:

JEREMIAH 38:14–40:6; 1 TIMOTHY 1:18–3:13;
PROVERBS 13:5–13

The light of the righteous rejoiceth:
but the lamp of the wicked shall be put out.

PROVERBS 13:9

Live a life for God in the world today, and others are sure to take notice. You'll stand out—whether it's at work, in school, on the bus, or wherever you go. People will see that you're different when you don't go along with the crowd—you'll be "full of light." Go on! Let your light shine today (Matthew 5:14).

Bible reading:

JEREMIAH 40:7–42:22; 1 TIMOTHY 3:14–4:10;
PROVERBS 13:14–21

*For bodily exercise profiteth little: but godliness is
profitable unto all things, having promise of the life
that now is, and of that which is to come.*

1 TIMOTHY 4:8

Millions of dollars and hours of effort are spent
on diet and exercise programs every year. Leading
a healthy lifestyle is important, but the truth is
that the body is a temporary shell for the Spirit.
God urges His children to spend time growing in
our faith as well. Unlike diet and exercise, Godlike
living has an eternal guarantee.

*Take heed unto thyself, and unto the doctrine;
continue in them: for in doing this thou shalt both
save thyself, and them that hear thee.*

1 TIMOTHY 4:16

———— ❖ ————

This promise was given by one church leader to another—but the principle applies to all of us. Other people notice when we as Christians believe the Bible and live our lives accordingly. And those who "hear" us—the folks who see our consistent Christian conduct and take it to heart—can be saved by calling on the Jesus we know and serve. And isn't that really what this life is all about?

Bible reading:

JEREMIAH 45–47; 1 TIMOTHY 5:17–6:21;
PROVERBS 14:1–6

But godliness with contentment is great gain.
1 TIMOTHY 6:6

When new "toys" are advertised on television, it's natural to crave them. We can take a tip from the apostle Paul, who knew what it was like to have it all—or nothing (Philippians 4:12). Greater happiness, he writes, is found by being happy with what you have than by spending money on things that take away from time with your heavenly Father (1 Timothy 6:8, 10).

Bible reading:

JEREMIAH 48:1–49:6; 2 TIMOTHY 1;
PROVERBS 14:7–22

*For God hath not given us the spirit of fear;
but of power, and of love, and of a sound mind.*

2 TIMOTHY 1:7

Toss your fears aside. That's what God wants you
to do. Fear doesn't come from Him—so we must
embrace the power, the love, and the wisdom
with which He has blessed us. Ask God today
to remove the fear from your spirit, so you can
fully experience the joy-filled life that's possible
through Him.

Bible reading:

JEREMIAH 49:7–50:16; 2 TIMOTHY 2;
PROVERBS 14:23–27

In meekness instructing those that oppose themselves;
if God peradventure will give them repentance
to the acknowledging of the truth.
2 TIMOTHY 2:25

Ultimately, it's not up to us to change the hearts of those who don't believe the way we do. God promises that if we go about witnessing in a gentle way, He is the One who can soften hard hearts. No need to be discouraged if it seems we just aren't able to reach others; God can work behind the scenes in ways we can't. So keep on reaching out to others with the Good News. . .and leave the rest up to God.

Bible reading:

JEREMIAH 50:17–51:14; 2 TIMOTHY 3;
PROVERBS 14:28–35

*All scripture is given by inspiration of God, and is
profitable for doctrine, for reproof, for correction,
for instruction in righteousness: that the man of God may
be perfect, thoroughly furnished unto all good works.*

2 TIMOTHY 3:16–17

❖ ⊰•⊱ ❖

Have you ever read a book that was so deeply
satisfying that it felt as though it was speaking
directly to you? The Bible can do just that. God's
Word is just as real and relevant today as it was two
thousand years ago. For Christians, God's Word
promises to supply everything they need to work
well for Him. Think of it as a letter penned by
God and delivered straight to you.

Bible reading:

JEREMIAH 51:15–64; 2 TIMOTHY 4; PROVERBS 15:1–9

A soft answer turneth away wrath:
but grievous words stir up anger.

PROVERBS 15:1

———————

Some of the Bible's promises, like those regarding heaven, have a long-term payoff. But others, like Proverbs 15:1, have a practical, everyday benefit. Since God created people, He knows what they're like—and He knows that angry words generate additional anger. Gentle answers are like water on a fire, cooling the heat and limiting the damage. Can you put this promise into practice today?

Bible reading:

JEREMIAH 52–LAMENTATIONS 1; TITUS 1:1–9;
PROVERBS 15:10–17

*Paul, a servant of God, and an apostle of Jesus
Christ, according to the faith of God's elect, and the
acknowledging of the truth which is after godliness;
in hope of eternal life, which God, that cannot lie,
promised before the world began.*

TITUS 1:1–2

❦

You've heard lots of people say, "I'm telling
the truth." But the truth mentioned in today's
scripture reading is the only truth that has eternal
impact. This "truth" refers to God's sacrifice
of His only Son for our sins (John 3:16). God
promises that if we believe and accept His gift,
we will have eternal life. Put your trust in God's
Word today.

*It is of the LORD's mercies that we are not consumed,
because his compassions fail not. They are new
every morning: great is thy faithfulness.*
LAMENTATIONS 3:22–23

Consider the renewal you get from the cleansing
water when you bathe. After a workout, or a tough
day at work, or a hot summer day, nothing feels
better than a relaxing shower. God's love and grace
renew with a cleansing power greater than any
shower. He faithfully provides renewing streams
to His children every morning of every day.

Bible reading:

LAMENTATIONS 3:39–5:22; TITUS 3;
PROVERBS 15:27–33

The LORD is far from the wicked:
but he heareth the prayer of the righteous.

PROVERBS 15:29

God promises to listen to us when we're "righteous." The other side of the coin is that sin in our lives breaks the fellowship we could enjoy with God. There are any number of ways to mess up—Peter once wrote that a man's prayers can be hindered if he just shows disrespect to his wife (1 Peter 3:7)—but consciously maintaining a close relationship with God brings countless benefits.

A man's heart deviseth his way:
but the LORD directeth his steps.

Proverbs 16:9

God has given us free will. We have the ability to make choices for our own lives—whether good or bad. So how can we be sure we're making the right choices? Ask God. His Word gives guidance and direction for each step we take (Proverbs 3:6). He will always lead us on the right path—guaranteed (Psalm 37:23).

Bible reading:

 EZEKIEL 3:22–5:17; HEBREWS 1:1–2:4;
PROVERBS 16:10–21

*The wise in heart shall be called prudent:
and the sweetness of the lips increaseth learning.*

PROVERBS 16:21

Have you ever been so enraged by injustice or blatant sin that all you wanted to do was shout and throw things? Your reaction may be a prodding of the Holy Spirit who is saying, "Hey, wait a second. God is not happy about this!" But it's in our reaction that God can be found. Confronting others in a calm and gentle way may allow them to see the truth, and you will honor God at the same time.

Bible reading:

Yet will I leave a remnant, that ye may have some
that shall escape the sword among the nations,
when ye shall be scattered through the countries.

EZEKIEL 6:8

Judgment day had come for the idol-worshipping people of Israel. Through the prophet Ezekiel, God promised to punish His chosen people for their disobedience—but to stay true to His earlier promises to Abraham and David, God also promised to save some of the people. How? By scattering them among the other nations. Look around today—Jewish people the world over confirm God's complete truthfulness.

Bible reading:

Ezekiel 8–10; Hebrews 3:1–4:3; Proverbs 17:1–5

Better is a dry morsel, and quietness therewith,
than an house full of sacrifices with strife.

Proverbs 17:1

"Anger management" has spawned an entire industry, with books to read and courses to take, all "guaranteed" to help control one's temper. How comforting it is to read these ancient words about our God: "But thou art a God ready to pardon, gracious and merciful, slow to anger, and of great kindness" (Nehemiah 9:17). To enter into God's presence is to come into a place of "peace and quiet."

Bible reading:

EZEKIEL 11–12; HEBREWS 4:4–5:10;
PROVERBS 17:6–12

Neither is there any creature that is not manifest in his sight: but all things are naked and opened unto the eyes of him with whom we have to do.

HEBREWS 4:13

We can hide our hearts from our spouses. We can hide our hearts from our friends. We can hide our hearts from our coworkers. But no matter how hard we try, we can't hide our hearts from God. He sees and knows everything about us—what we think, what we feel, what we do. And yet He still loves us (Ephesians 2:4–7)!

*That ye be not slothful, but followers of them who
through faith and patience inherit the promises.*

Hebrews 6:12

Life sometimes makes our Christian faith seem all
but impossible. God knows this. He's also given
us examples of people who endured in their faith
despite extreme circumstances—Noah, Abraham,
Moses, Mary, Paul. God asks for faithfulness and
guarantees a reward in return: eternal life in
heaven.

Bible reading:

EZEKIEL 15:1–16:43; HEBREWS 7;
PROVERBS 17:23–28

A foolish son is a grief to his father,
and bitterness to her that bare him.

PROVERBS 17:25

❖

Nobody likes this kind of Bible promise, but it's in God's Word for a reason. When we do wrong, we hurt other people, especially those closest to us. Remember God's promise of sowing and reaping—we get back what we put into life (Galatians 6:7–8). Be wise, and bring joy and blessing to the people you love!

EZEKIEL 16:44–17:24; HEBREWS 8:1–9:10;
PROVERBS 18:1–7

For I will be merciful to their unrighteousness,
and their sins and their iniquities will
I remember no more.

HEBREWS 8:12

It's easy to point out someone else's shortcomings, isn't it? But we are called to love and forgive others despite their mistakes (Mark 11:25–26). Follow God's example, as He promises to continue to love us even though we fail Him. And He forgives us every time we ask—never to bring it up again. Ask Him to help you extend forgiveness to someone today.

Bible reading:

Ezekiel 18–19; Hebrews 9:11–28;
Proverbs 18:8–17

But if the wicked will turn from all his sins that he hath committed, and keep all my statutes, and do that which is lawful and right, he shall surely live, he shall not die. All his transgressions that he hath committed, they shall not be mentioned unto him: in his righteousness that he hath done he shall live.

Ezekiel 18:21–22

Humans strive for youthfulness through diet, exercise, and cosmetics—all in an effort to delay aging and death. God offers the ultimate antiaging guarantee: eternal life. In heaven there will be no over-the-hill birthday celebrations, no uncertainty about the future, no wrinkles, no hair loss, no death.

Bible reading:

EZEKIEL 20; HEBREWS 10:1–25;
PROVERBS 18:18–24

A man's belly shall be satisfied with the fruit of his mouth; and with the increase of his lips shall he be filled.

PROVERBS 18:20

Think about the imagery of this verse for minute: If bitter, awful words come from your mouth, you'll feel that bitter awfulness in the pit of your stomach. If you're speaking sweet, healthy words, that's what the rest of your system will register. What more do we need to say about this promise?

Bible reading:

EZEKIEL 21–22; HEBREWS 10:26–39;
PROVERBS 19:1–8

*For ye have need of patience, that, after ye have done
the will of God, ye might receive the promise.*

HEBREWS 10:36

We often ask God for things, even though we may
not be living according to His will. We continue to
disobey Him; but when we have a need, we selfishly
call on Him and yet wonder why nothing seems to
be going right in our lives. God doesn't guarantee
us a trouble-free life, but He does promise to bless
our lives and fulfill His promise to us if we will
obey His commands (Deuteronomy 5:29, 6:18).

Bible reading.

But without faith it is impossible to please him: for he that cometh to God must believe that he is, and that he is a rewarder of them that diligently seek him.

HEBREWS 11:6

Faith pleases God. It's that simple. He's not a holy Santa Claus who simply wants to hear our requests; He wants our trust and belief that He exists and is able to supply our every want and need. When we follow through with our faith and seek Him, He'll bless our lives beyond our wildest dreams.

Bible reading:

EZEKIEL 24–26; HEBREWS 11:32–40;
PROVERBS 19:15–21

*He that keepeth the commandment
keepeth his own soul.*

PROVERBS 19:16

Which of God's promises can be bigger than this
one? By keeping God's Word—by studying and
applying it to our lives—we keep our souls. What
does that mean? We preserve and protect them,
from the destruction of sin and hell. In Jesus'
own statement, "I know that his commandment
is life everlasting" (John 12:50).

Bible reading:

EZEKIEL 27–28; HEBREWS 12:1–13;
PROVERBS 19:22–29

Wherefore seeing we also are compassed about with so great a cloud of witnesses, let us lay aside every weight, and the sin which doth so easily beset us, and let us run with patience the race that is set before us.

HEBREWS 12:1

For those who wonder if they could run around the block, the many references to running in the Bible can be daunting. Yet, as believers who know that the finish tape ends in heaven, tying on those spiritual sneakers can be an exercise in trusting God's promise of eternal life. Like Paul, one day we can rejoice that "I have fought a good fight, I have finished my course, I have kept the faith" (2 Timothy 4:7).

The just man walketh in his integrity:
his children are blessed after him.

PROVERBS 20:7

Our lifestyles. Our morals. Our values. Our priorities. However we choose to live, we are affecting the lives of our children. We are called to teach our children God's ways and to live our lives so that they may learn Christlike behavior from our actions (Isaiah 54:13). If we obey God and walk closely with Him, He promises that our children will be happy.

Bible reading:

EZEKIEL 31–32; HEBREWS 13; PROVERBS 20:19–24

Say not thou, I will recompense evil;
but wait on the LORD, and he shall save thee.
PROVERBS 20:22

We say we want justice, and we want it now. Earthly justice, however, is sometimes a masquerade for revenge. When someone wrongs us somehow, our immediate response is retaliation—an eye-for-eye and tooth-for-tooth mentality. God tells us to have patience when we're wronged. He'll deliver justice that's better than any revenge we can dole out.

Bible reading:

Let no man say when he is tempted, I am tempted
of God: for God cannot be tempted with evil,
neither tempteth he any man.

JAMES 1:13

❖ ·■· ❖

God is always good. Though He may allow you
to experience some tough things, He'll never try
to trip you up. Since He can't be tempted to do
wrong, He won't tempt you to do wrong either.
In fact, He's promised that "God is faithful, who
will not suffer you to be tempted above that ye
are able; but will with the temptation also make
a way to escape, that ye may be able to bear it"
(1 Corinthians 10:13).

Bible reading

EZEKIEL 34:11–36:15; JAMES 2; PROVERBS 21:1–8

I will feed my flock, and I will cause them to lie down,
saith the Lord GOD. I will seek that which was lost,
and bring again that which was driven away, and will
bind up that which was broken, and will strengthen
that which was sick: but I will destroy the fat and
the strong; I will feed them with judgment.

EZEKIEL 34:15–16

God is our Good Shepherd. When we are hungry, He will feed us. When we are tired, He will give us rest. When we lose our way, He will find us again. When we are hurting, He will tend to our wounds. And when we are sick, He will infuse us with His strength. No matter how weak you are in spirit, He will never leave you lost and alone. Reach out to Him and allow Him to envelop you in the shelter of His love.

Bible reading:

EZEKIEL 36:16–37:28; JAMES 3; PROVERBS 21:9–18

*And the fruit of righteousness is sown
in peace of them that make peace.*

JAMES 3:18

A farmer will never sow a kernel of corn and reap a thistle bush. When he plants good, quality seeds, he'll have a harvest of good, quality produce. That's similar to what God promises His children who sow peace about them. Peace planted in situations and lives around you will yield righteousness and goodness—crops that glorify the Creator!

Bible reading:

EZEKIEL 38–39; JAMES 4:1–5:6; PROVERBS 21:19–24

*Whoso keepeth his mouth and his tongue
keepeth his soul from troubles.*

PROVERBS 21:23

Here's one of those really practical promises of
the Bible. Watch your mouth—be careful what you
say—and you'll avoid a lot of trouble. Easier said
than done, perhaps. . .but that's where God's Holy
Spirit comes in. Remember the fruit of the Spirit
in Galatians 5:22–23? The last one mentioned is
temperance, or self-control. Control your speech.
Doesn't that sound better than saying something
you'll regret?

Bible reading:

EZEKIEL 40; JAMES 5:7–20; PROVERBS 21:25–31

The effectual fervent prayer of a
righteous man availeth much.

JAMES 5:16

God promises that our prayers are packed with spiritual "punch" if our lives are right with Him. While He hears *all* prayer, it's comforting to know that we can have a bigger impact if we are living in obedience to Him. Thank God today for the awesome effect we can have with our prayer lives if we are faithful Christians.

Bible reading:

EZEKIEL 41:1–43:12; 1 PETER 1:1–12;
PROVERBS 22:1–9

Whom having not seen, ye love; in whom,
though now ye see him not, yet believing,
ye rejoice with joy unspeakable and full of glory.

1 PETER 1:8

Only a select group of people ever got to interact with Jesus during His thirty-three years on earth. The good news is that present-day Christians can express the same love that first-century Christians held for the Messiah—all it takes is belief and trust. Our love for Jesus leads to a joy that's so great that words cannot describe it.

Bible reading:

EZEKIEL 43:13–44:31; 1 PETER 1:13–2:3;
PROVERBS 22:10–23

---

*And if ye call on the Father, who without respect of
persons judgeth according to every man's work.*

1 PETER 1:17

There's an old saying that goes like this: "The
ground is level at the foot of the cross." What it
means is that anyone and everyone needs Jesus,
and anyone and everyone can come to God
through Him. God doesn't care if you're rich or
poor, healthy or sick, man or woman or child.
He loved everyone enough to send Jesus—and
promises to accept all who come through Him.

Bible reading:

EZEKIEL 45—46; 1 PETER 2:4—17;
PROVERBS 22:24—29

Be not thou one of them that strike hands,
or of them that are sureties for debts.
PROVERBS 22:26

The Bible is a very practical book, and this verse tells us not to promise our own lives and goods for other people's debt. In modern terms, that's cosigning a loan—and it can put you in a real bind, according to the next verse: "If thou hast nothing to pay, why should he take away thy bed from under thee?" (Proverbs 22:27). Look to the Bible for guidance on spiritual matters. . .but also for the practical questions of life.

*[Jesus,] who his own self bare our sins in his own body
on the tree, that we, being dead to sins, should live
unto righteousness: by whose stripes ye were healed.*

1 PETER 2:24

A strange concept. . .that the wounds of another—
Jesus Christ—could actually heal us. But that's what
God's Word says. Jesus was wounded and ultimately
died for our transgressions (Isaiah 53:5). And
through His sacrifice—His promise—we are able to
experience an abundant life—and be freed from the
punishment of sin forever (Hebrews 9:28).

*For he that will love life, and see good days, let him
refrain his tongue from evil, and his lips that they
speak no guile: Let him eschew evil, and do good;
let him seek peace, and ensue it.*

1 PETER 3:10–11

Want joy? Want a happy life? God promises these
things to those who restrain themselves from
indulging in gossip and sin. Go after goodness
and peace, He commands, and He'll deliver on
His promise.

Bible reading:

DANIEL 2:24–3:30; 1 PETER 5; PROVERBS 23:17–25

Bring me in before the king,
and I will shew unto the king the interpretation.

DANIEL 2:24

❖━━━━❖━━❖━━━━❖

This was a promise from a condemned man. Daniel and the other "wise men of Babylon" faced a death penalty if they couldn't tell King Nebuchadnezzar what his dream meant. . .after telling him what his dream *was*. But Daniel wasn't desperately trying to buy time. He trusted God, who told him both the king's dream and its interpretation. Though we'll probably never be in such a dramatic situation ourselves, we can still trust God for all the wisdom we need in life.

Bible reading:

DANIEL 4; 2 PETER 1; PROVERBS 23:26–35

*How great are his signs! and how mighty are his wonders!
his kingdom is an everlasting kingdom, and his
dominion is from generation to generation.*

DANIEL 4:3

No matter who we are or where we come from,
God's Word—and His promises—apply to us. Rich
or poor, man or woman, beautiful or plain. From
ancient history to today, His Word stands timeless.
We can count on our Father, our Friend, to keep
His promises. We never have to wonder. We never
have to question. We never have to worry. All we
must do is believe.

Bible reading:

My son, eat thou honey, because it is good; and the honeycomb, which is sweet to thy taste: So shall the knowledge of wisdom be unto thy soul: when thou hast found it, then there shall be a reward, and thy expectation shall not be cut off.

PROVERBS 24:13–14

God's wisdom may be well beyond our grasp, but He still encourages His children to seek for and grow in wisdom. God says His wisdom is as sweet and soothing to the soul as honey is to the taste buds. God guarantees His wisdom can be the nourishment we need to sustain us and give hope for today and tomorrow.

Bible reading:

Daniel 6:1–7:14; 2 Peter 3; Proverbs 24:19–27

The Lord is not slack concerning his promise,
as some men count slackness; but is longsuffering to
us-ward, not willing that any should perish,
but that all should come to repentance.

2 Peter 3:9

What promise is Peter describing? The promised return of Jesus Christ. Many people question it: "Where is the promise of his coming? for since the fathers fell asleep, all things continue as they were from the beginning of the creation" (2 Peter 3:4). But Peter reminds us that time is different with God: "Beloved, be not ignorant of this one thing, that one day is with the Lord as a thousand years, and a thousand years as one day" (2 Peter 3:8). God will keep His promise. He's just giving people more time to turn to Him.

Bible reading:

DANIEL 7:15–8:27; 1 JOHN 1:1–2:17;
PROVERBS 24:28–34

God is light, and in him is no darkness at all.
1 JOHN 1:5

When your life seems overcome by darkness, there is hope. Place God in the center of your life, and He will lift your spirit. He will give you the strength and courage you need to overcome even the most challenging obstacles (Psalm 31:24). Find the faith that you need for life: look to the light.

*And now, little children, abide in him; that,
when he shall appear, we may have confidence,
and not be ashamed before him at his coming.*

1 JOHN 2:28

God didn't create humans to be entirely self-
reliant. He knows that we need Him, even when
we don't realize it ourselves. John reminds us of
our reliance on God by telling us to live with His
help. By relying on Him to help us day to day and
in the difficult times, our relationship with the
Creator is strengthened.

Bible reading:

DANIEL 11–12; 1 JOHN 3:1–12; PROVERBS 25:13–17

*Beloved, now are we the sons of God, and it doth
not yet appear what we shall be: but we know that,
when he shall appear, we shall be like him;
for we shall see him as he is.*

1 JOHN 3:2

Most of us have days when we just don't like
ourselves very much. Our appearance, our health,
our attitudes, our temptations—so many issues
trouble us. But God has promised Christians
a day when all our problems will be over. We'll
actually be like Jesus—perfect and complete in
every way. "And every man that hath this hope
in him purifieth himself, even as he is pure"
(1 John 3:3).

Bible reading:

It is not good to eat much honey:
so for men to search their own glory is not glory.

PROVERBS 25:27

Substitute "chocolate" for "honey," and everyone can understand the first half of this verse. God's promise is that too much of the sweet stuff can make us sick—just like the pursuit of personal recognition can hurt us. Follow the apostle Peter's advice, instead: "Humble yourselves therefore under the mighty hand of God, that he may exalt you in due time" (I Peter 5:6).

❧ *Bible reading:* ❧

HOSEA 4–6; 1 JOHN 4:17–5:21; PROVERBS 26:1–16

*For whatsoever is born of God overcometh the world:
and this is the victory that overcometh the
world, even our faith.*

1 JOHN 5:4

Does sin have control over your life? Do you have daily struggles with temptations so great, you're not sure you can overcome them? God says that, as His children, we have "the victory that overcometh the world." And that power is through our faith (Romans 6:14). Ask God to strengthen your faith today, and thank Him for providing you a way to overcome sin in your life (1 Corinthians 10:13).

Bible reading:

HOSEA 7–10; 2 JOHN; PROVERBS 26:17–21

He that abideth in the doctrine of Christ,
he hath both the Father and the Son.

2 JOHN 1:9

Jesus' teachings came with a simple message: "If you're in with me, you're in with my Father." For His disciples, this was a radical thought. Until the time of Christ, the Hebrews considered God a lofty ruler who could only be approached through ritual and tradition. Jesus offers a real relationship to Christians—not only with the Son, but with the Father as well.

Bible reading:

HOSEA 11–14; 3 JOHN; PROVERBS 26:22–27:9

*Which have borne witness of thy charity before the
church: whom if thou bring forward on their
journey after a godly sort, thou shalt do well.*

3 JOHN 1:6

Hospitality is good for everyone—especially for
those doing the hosting. God has promised good
to Christians who help out other Christians. And
He's promised good to Christians who help out
"strangers"—people not already in our circles. As
we bless others with our kindness, God is blessed. . .
and He blesses us in turn.

Bible reading:

JOEL 1:1–2:17; JUDE; PROVERBS 27:10–17

Turn unto the LORD your God: for he is gracious and merciful, slow to anger, and of great kindness, and repenteth him of the evil.

JOEL 2:13

Have you ever found yourself so far out of sync with God that you felt you could never make things right with Him again? God's Word says that we can always return to Him. His love can bridge even the deepest chasm and bring you back into a close relationship with Him (Ephesians 2:4–7).

Bible reading:

JOEL 2:18–3:21; REVELATION 1:1–2:11;
PROVERBS 27:18–27

*Blessed is he that readeth, and they that hear
the words of this prophecy, and keep those
things which are written therein.*

REVELATION 1:3

Many people avoid the book of Revelation, with its
mysterious prophecies and images of destruction.
But, right off the bat, it promises happiness to
anyone who will read it, hear it read, and obey
what it says. With an offer like that, why wouldn't
you study Revelation?

Bible reading:

AMOS 1:1–4:5; REVELATION 2:12–29;
PROVERBS 28:1–8

Better is the poor that walketh in his uprightness,
than he that is perverse in his ways, though he be rich.
PROVERBS 28:6

In a world that worships money, this Bible promise seems crazy. It's better to be poor? Well, yes. . .if you're walking in honor. Do what's right, every time, and God will provide the most amazing payback—perhaps here on this earth, but for sure in heaven to come.

Bible reading:

AMOS 4:6–6:14; REVELATION 3; PROVERBS 28:9–16

Behold, I stand at the door, and knock: if any man
hear my voice, and open the door, I will come in to
him, and will sup with him, and he with me.

REVELATION 3:20

God is waiting for you. He's knocking on the door
of your heart right now. Invite Him in. . .and
open your heart to everything He has to offer.
Prepare to be infused with an overabundance of
peace and joy that only He can bring into your
life (John 15:11).

Bible reading:

AMOS 7–9; REVELATION 4:1–5:5;
PROVERBS 28:17–24

He that tilleth his land shall have plenty of bread:
but he that followeth after vain persons
shall have poverty enough.

PROVERBS 28:19

Hard work reaps rewards. God shows this throughout scripture, and Jesus teaches it in His parables. An honest day's work yields fair pay, and honest transactions are blessed by God. The flip side of this promise is that a lazy person who squanders his time will lose whatever blessings and riches he may acquire. Learn from this promise— now get to work!

Bible reading:

OBADIAH–JONAH; REVELATION 5:6–14;
PROVERBS 28:25–28

*But I will sacrifice unto thee with the voice
of thanksgiving; I will pay that that I have
vowed. Salvation is of the LORD.*

JONAH 2:9

For promises made in strange places, this one
wins the prize: Jonah spoke these words inside a
fish's stomach. A disobedient prophet, trying to
run from God, Jonah had three days and nights
in a living prison cell to consider his spiritual
obligations. . .and this prayer is what resulted. The
point for us? Don't slip so far into disobedience
that God uses extreme measures to get your
attention!

Bible reading:

Micah 1:1–4:5; Revelation 6:1–7:8;
Proverbs 29:1–8

*Nation shall not lift up a sword against nation,
neither shall they learn war any more.*

Micah 4:3

One day, after Jesus comes again, a new kingdom
will be established on a new earth (Revelation 21:1).
In this new kingdom, not only will wars cease, but
there will be no crying, no death, and no pain
(Revelation 21:4). And that's not just the opinion
of some hermit or cult leader. . .that's a promise
from God Himself.

Bible reading:

Micah 4:6–7:20; Revelation 7:9–8:13;
Proverbs 29:9–14

*For the Lamb which is in the midst of the throne
shall feed them, and shall lead them unto living
fountains of waters: and God shall wipe
away all tears from their eyes.*

REVELATION 7:17

One day, as we enter eternity with our brothers
and sisters in Christ, we will be freed from all sin,
sickness, and suffering. Our Good Shepherd,
Jesus Christ, will take all earthly woes and remove
them from us—permanently. Never again will we
shed a tear. Never again will we feel pain. Never
again will we experience loss. All we'll know is
joy and peace as we praise and worship the Lord
for eternity.

Bible reading:

A man's pride shall bring him low:
but honour shall uphold the humble in spirit.

PROVERBS 29:23

For most of us, it's difficult to admit when we're wrong or that we need help. But God asks us to humble ourselves and put pride aside. God guarantees honor to His children who can look at a situation and consider the needs of others before themselves—a direct command of scripture (Philippians 2:3).

The kingdoms of this world are become the
kingdoms of our Lord, and of his Christ;
and he shall reign for ever and ever.

REVELATION 11:15

Watch the evening news, and you'll probably become depressed. We live in a troubled world, full of bad people and bad situations. But the day is coming when Jesus will rule with perfect justice. Everything bad will be done away with; life will be ideal. And His reign will last forever. Now that's a promise worth remembering!

Bible reading:

ZEPHANIAH; REVELATION 12; PROVERBS 30:1–6

Every word of God is pure: he is a shield unto
them that put their trust in him.

PROVERBS 30:5

———————

It's human nature to question whether someone is being truthful. We know from past experiences that some people are unable to be honest and forthright. It's refreshing that there is Someone whom we can believe—at all times—for "every word" of His has been proven. Not once has He been dishonest or indirect (1 Kings 8:56). Place your trust in Him today.

*And I heard a voice from heaven saying unto me,
Write, Blessed are the dead which die in the Lord
from henceforth: Yea, saith the Spirit, that they may
rest from their labours; and their works do follow them.*

REVELATION 14:13

✦

Some of God's greatest promises are wrapped up
in the guarantee of eternal life for His children.
He promises no more death, no more sickness,
no more tears—but it's not just the absence of bad
things that will make heaven so wonderful. Heaven
will be a state of pure happiness as we worship the
King of kings who humbled Himself to be born
to a poor Jewish couple in a barn.

Bible reading:

ZECHARIAH 1–4; REVELATION 14:14–16:3;
PROVERBS 30:17–20

*And the LORD shall inherit Judah his portion in the
holy land, and shall choose Jerusalem again.*

ZECHARIAH 2:12

Modern Jerusalem is a troubled place. Violence, terrorism, and war have plagued the city for generations. But God still loves His ancient capital, and promises that He will make it the center of government of an ideal new world. Next time you hear Jerusalem mentioned in the news, think ahead to an age of perfect peace and prosperity—ruled by Jesus Himself.

Bible reading:

ZECHARIAH 5–8; REVELATION 16:4–21;
PROVERBS 30:21–28

*Behold, I come as a thief. Blessed is he that
watcheth, and keepeth his garments.*
REVELATION 16:15

Although we know Christ will return one day,
it often slips to the backs of our minds as we
walk through life. But He wants us to wait in
anticipation—to always be ready. For He says He
will come "as a thief." There will be no grand
announcement, no set date or time for His return.
So prepare your heart, and wait expectantly.

Bible reading:

Zechariah 9–11; Revelation 17:1–18:8;
Proverbs 30:29–33

*The Lamb shall overcome them: for he is Lord of lords,
and King of kings: and they that are with him
are called, and chosen, and faithful.*

REVELATION 17:14

❖

Satan will be vanquished. Jesus is and will be
King of all. Why? Because He was and is and
will be. There's no guarantee greater than that.
He deserves our honor and praise and gratitude
because He thought enough of each of us to offer
grace. He calls us His chosen and faithful ones.
Hallelujah!

Bible reading:

ZECHARIAH 12–14; REVELATION 18:9–24;
PROVERBS 31:1–9

There shall be no more utter destruction.

ZECHARIAH 14:11

Ever since Adam and Eve blew it in the Garden of Eden, humanity has lived under a curse. We work hard, get old, and die. We experience disease, accidents, and emotional trials. Life becomes, at times, very hard. But someday, in God's good time, that will all change. The curse will be lifted, and God will make everything new (Revelation 21:5)!

Bible reading:

MALACHI 1–2; REVELATION 19–20;
PROVERBS 31:10–17

Who can find a virtuous woman?
for her price is far above rubies.
PROVERBS 31:10

A good wife, a faithful husband, a long-lasting marriage. . .these are all gifts from God. From the moment Eve was created, God wanted marriage to be a permanent blessing and a unifying force in an often fragmented society (Genesis 2:24). God honors marriage (Hebrews 13:4), and He blesses wives and husbands who seek His will and His promises.

Bible reading:

MALACHI 3–4; REVELATION 21–22;
PROVERBS 31:18–31

For I am the LORD, I change not.
MALACHI 3:6

Life is full of change. People change. Careers change. Our circumstances change. Our opinions change. In a world where there is no consistency, what a blessing we have in this promise that God has given to us: "I am the LORD, I change not." His Word is guaranteed—now and forever. Amen!

SCRIPTURE INDEX

Check out More Editions of *The Bible Promise Book®*

The Bible Promise Book® for Hope and Healing

Featuring dozens of timely topics—including Addiction, Rest, Peace, Forgiveness, Eternity, God's Love, Salvation, God's Power, Prayer, Comfort, and Perseverance—readers will find hundreds of verses from God's Word that will speak to their daily needs. *The Bible Promise Book® for Hope and Healing* is ideal for personal use and for ministries.

Paperback / 978-1-63058-860-1 / $5.99

The Bible Promise Book® Devotional

For more than 30 years, *The Bible Promise Book®* has blessed millions of readers. This daily devotional highlights more than 40 *Bible Promise Book®* topics from A to Z—from Adversity and Gratitude to Forgiveness, Patience, Salvation, and Wisdom. Perfect for daily quiet time or Bible study, *The Bible Promise Book® Devotional* is perfect for readers of all ages.

Paperback / 978-1-68322-181-4 / $7.99